A WORKBOOK FOR SELF-STUDY

READING & WRITING
JAPANESE

A Beginner's Guide to Hiragana, Katakana and Kanji

by Eriko Sato

Illustrations by Anna Sato

TUTTLE Publishing

Tokyo | Rutland, Vermont | Singapore

Contents

PART THREE   Kanji

Introduction

Modern Japanese is written horizontally or vertically by combining three types of scripts. These are kanji (漢字), Chinese characters adapted to Japan, and two sets of phonetic symbols called kana (仮名), which are hiragana (平仮名) and katakana (片仮名). These three types of scripts are mixed not only within sentences, but also within words. For example, the Japanese word that means "eraser" (*keshigomu*) is written as follows:

The first element of the word, 消, is a kanji character representing the concept of "erasing." The second is the hiragana character し (*shi*). It represents the sound "shi," the inflectional part of the Japanese verb *kesu*, which means "to erase." The third and fourth elements, ゴム (*gomu*), are katakana. Together, they represent the sound of the word "gum," loaned from English.

Hiragana and katakana each have 46 basic characters in modern Japanese, and the average Japanese person can read 1,000 to 2,000 kanji characters. However, if you learn the 50 most frequently used kanji characters and develop a thorough understanding of how kanji are formed and used, you can understand about 30 percent of the texts in Japanese magazines. Building a solid foundation is the key to success! This workbook lets you master all hiragana and katakana characters and the 50 simplest, most basic, and/or most frequently used kanji characters, along with over 500 vocabulary words.

How to use this book

This book has three parts:

- Part One: Hiragana
- Part Two: Katakana
- Part Three: Kanji

Each part consists of fifteen short lessons. Most lessons are only two pages long and are placed on facing pages, except when there is an extensive instruction or explanation. Each of the first ten lessons in each part introduces just three to five new characters. This makes it easy for you to focus on the lessons one at a time.

Romanization is used as the preliminary pronunciation guide in Part One and partially in Part Two. You won't see any romanization after that. Hiragana characters are used as the pronunciation guide in Part Three. Although the focus in Part Three is on kanji, practice exercises include a mixture of hiragana, katakana and kanji. Thus, it is essential to finish Part One completely before starting Parts Two and Three.

This book is accompanied by online audio recordings for almost all the exercises, which can be accessed via the link on page 12. As you learn the characters, you can learn more than 500 basic Japanese vocabulary words with authentic pronunciation. To help you learn vocabulary easily, words are introduced in thematic groups wherever possible.

Before you begin, let's talk a little about the history and usage conventions of the Japanese writing system.

The history of the Japanese writing system

The ancient Japanese did not have their own scripts; they borrowed Chinese characters. The first text from Japan dates to the fifth century. During the sixth and seventh centuries, Chinese Buddhism was brought to Japan via Korea, making it necessary for the Japanese to read a large number of Chinese texts, or *kanbun* (漢文). These were read in one of two ways: *ondoku* (音読, sound reading) or *kundoku* (訓読, gloss reading). *Kanbun-ondoku* (漢文音読), the sound reading of Chinese texts, involved reading sentences with their original pronunciation, word order and grammar, just as any second-language learner of Chinese would do. On the other hand, *kanbun-kundoku* (漢文訓読), the gloss reading of Chinese texts, involved reading the Japanese translation for Chinese words and sentences, a kind of instant mental translation of Chinese texts to Japanese.

Chinese and Japanese have very different vocabulary words, grammar and word order. For *kanbun-kundoku* reading, the reader had to quickly revise the word order, add needed Japanese particles and inflectional endings and replace many words with Japanese translation equivalents—all accomplished mentally and verbalized instantaneously. To facilitate this acrobatic mental translation, the ancient Japanese often used *kunten* (訓点), a system of guiding marks for altering Chinese sentences into Japanese in terms of grammar and pronunciation along with gloss annotations.

In *kanbun-kundoku* readings, it wasn't always easy to come up with an equivalent Japanese word for each Chinese word, which led to neo-borrowings from Chinese, where Chinese words were read with a Japanese accent. *Kanbun-kundoku* reading led to the Japanese assigning one or more pronunciations to each kanji. The pronunciation of a kanji character based on the vocalized Japanese translation equivalent is called *kun'yomi* (訓読み). The pronunciation of a kanji character based on the approximation of the original Chinese pronunciation is called *on'yomi* (音読み). For example, the kanji character 山 (mountain) is read as **yama** in *kun'yomi* and as **san** in *on'yomi*.

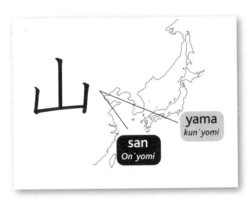

Kanbun-kundoku reading resulted in the creation of numerous loan words from Chinese. The words written in kanji and pronounced with their *on'yomi* have been called *kango* (漢語), or Sino-Japanese vocabulary. The *kunten* annotation method employed in the *kanbun-kundoku* practice contributed to the development of kana characters.

How about writing? The ancient Japanese initially used kanji exclusively in writing texts because there were no other scripts. In some places in a sentence, they would use kanji based on meaning; in other places they would use kanji based on sound—this sound-based writing system was called *manyōgana* (万葉仮名). For example, the Japanese word *yama* (mountain) could be written with the kanji 山 for its meaning, because this character means "mountain" in Chinese, but it could also be written with a sequence of two kanji characters—for example, 夜麻, 野麻 or 也麻—whose combined pronunciation is *ya-ma*. The strange part is that these kanji characters are totally unrelated to the idea of "mountain": 夜 (*ya*) means "night"; 麻 (*ma*) means "hemp"; 野 (*ya*) means "field"; and 也 (*ya*) means "to be." The following poem, found in Japan's oldest literary anthology, the *Manyōshū* (万葉集), includes the word "mountain" (*yama*) three times, written as 山 or 夜麻:

安之比奇能 山行之可婆 山之人乃和礼尓依志米之 夜麻都刀曾許礼
　　　　　yama　　　**yama**　　　　　　　　　　**yama**

Thanks to *manyōgana*, the ancient Japanese could write down their feelings to be read by us today, some 1,300 years later. However, writing and reading in *manyōgana* was cumbersome and confusing at times, because a character might be used for its meaning or for its sound. Although *manyōgana* was used until the twelfth century, in the ninth century Buddhist monks created two sets of syllable-based phonograms—hiragana (平仮名, plain kana) and katakana (片仮名, fragment kana)—by graphically reducing selected *manyōgana*. Hiragana is a set of simplified *manyōgana* written in cursive, whereas katakana is a set of selected partial *manyōgana*. For example, the hiragana か (**ka**) and the katakana カ (**ka**) were both developed from the kanji 加 (**ka**), but か is the simplified whole kanji 加, whereas カ is a component of that kanji. In some cases, the hiragana and katakana characters for the same sound were developed from different kanji characters.

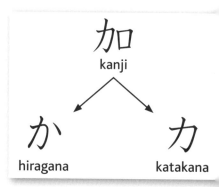

The following table lists hiragana and katakana characters derived from *manyōgana*, along with the source characters (rendered in gray):

n	w-	r-	y-	m-	h-	n-	t-	s-	k-		
ん 无	わ 和	ら 良	や 也	ま 末	は 波	な 奈	た 太	さ 左	か 加	あ 安	**-a**
ン	ワ 和	ラ 良	ヤ 也	マ 末	ハ 八	ナ 奈	タ 多	サ 散	カ 加	ア 阿	
		り 利		み 美	ひ 比	に 仁	ち 知	し 之	き 幾	い 以	**-i**
		リ 利		ミ 三	ヒ 比	ニ 二	チ 千	シ 之	キ 幾	イ 伊	
		る 留	ゆ 由	む 武	ふ 不	ぬ 奴	つ 川	す 寸	く 久	う 宇	**-u**
		ル 流	ユ 由	ム 牟	フ 不	ヌ 奴	ツ 州	ス 須	ク 久	ウ 宇	
		れ 礼		め 女	へ 部	ね 祢	て 天	せ 世	け 計	え 衣	**-e**
		レ 礼		メ 女	ヘ 部	ネ 祢	テ 天	セ 世	ケ 介	エ 江	
	を 遠	ろ 呂	よ 与	も 毛	ほ 保	の 乃	と 止	そ 曽	こ 己	お 於	**-o**
	ヲ 乎	ロ 呂	ヨ 与	モ 毛	ホ 保	ノ 乃	ト 止	ソ 曽	コ 己	オ 於	

You will notice that some hiragana/katakana pairs that look similar tend to have the same source kanji. The invention of kana enabled the Japanese to straightforwardly and easily write any Japanese sentence as it would be spoken in Japanese. In the Heian period (794–1185), a literary genre called "kana literature" emerged. The *Tale of Genji* (源氏物語, *Genji monogatari*) is an example of this genre. From the middle of the Heian period, *kanji-kana* mixed writing (漢字仮名交じり文, *kanji-kana majiribun*) emerged. In these texts, content words were mainly written in kanji, while grammatical particles and inflectional endings were written either in katakana or hiragana.

In the Meiji era (1868–1912), there were some movements to abolish kanji and use only kana or romanization (ローマ字, *rōmaji*), but they failed. However, the inventory of kanji characters and their readings have been reviewed and revised from time to time since the Meiji era.

Romanization, or rōmaji, means rendering Japanese words in the roman alphabet, and was first used by Portuguese traders and missionaries who came to Japan in the seventeenth century. The romanization system based on English that is most prevalent in Japan is Hepburn romanization. This system is attributed to the American missionary James Hepburn (1815–1911), who created it in the process of compiling the first Japanese-English dictionary in 1867.

Often, in romanized Japanese, especially in language-learning texts like this one, a long vowel is represented by a bar, called a macron, on top of that vowel. For example, *obāsan* (grandmother) has a long vowel whereas *obasan* (aunt) doesn't.

Japan's current writing system

Currently, kanji is used to represent words and names from Japanese and Chinese culture; katakana is used to represent words and names from non-Chinese foreign culture; and hiragana is used to specify grammatical particles, suffixes, prefixes, sentence-endings, and words and names in Japanese that are not covered by kanji or katakana. Rōmaji characters are used on signs at airports and train stations to assist foreign travelers.

As of 2010, there are 2,136 kanji characters listed as *jōyō* kanji (常用漢字, daily-use kanji) by the Japanese Ministry of Education. There are 46 basic hiragana and 46 basic katakana listed in common syllabary tables like the one below (hiragana on the left and katakana on the right):

n (n)	wa (wah)	ra (rah)	ya (yah)	ma (mah)	ha (hah)	na (nah)	ta (tah)	sa (sah)	ka (kah)	a (ah)
ん ン	わ ワ	ら ラ	や ヤ	ま マ	は ハ	な ナ	た タ	さ サ	か カ	あ ア
		ri (ree)		mi (mee)	hi (hee)	ni (nee)	chi (chee)	shi (shee)	ki (kee)	i (ee)
		り リ		み ミ	ひ ヒ	に ニ	ち チ	し シ	き キ	い イ
		ru (roo)	yu (yoo)	mu (moo)	fu (foo)	nu (noo)	tsu (tsoo)	su (soo)	ku (koo)	u (oo)
		る ル	ゆ ユ	む ム	ふ フ	ぬ ヌ	つ ツ	す ス	く ク	う ウ
		re (reh)		me (meh)	he (heh)	ne (neh)	te (teh)	se (seh)	ke (keh)	e (eh)
		れ レ		め メ	へ ヘ	ね ネ	て テ	せ セ	け ケ	え エ
	(w)o ([w]oh)	ro (roh)	yo (yoh)	mo (moh)	ho (hoh)	no (noh)	to (toh)	so (soh)	ko (koh)	o (oh)
	を ヲ	ろ ロ	よ ヨ	も モ	ほ ホ	の ノ	と ト	そ ソ	こ コ	お オ

You'll learn how to read and write these kana characters in Part One and Part Two of this book. Then, in Part Three, you'll learn 50 basic kanji characters.

Additional background on kanji

Kanji characters are slightly more complex in terms of their structure and usage. The following is an overview of their internal structures, the way they are used in Japanese writing systems, and the way they are combined to create new meanings.

The formation of Chinese characters

Kanji are Chinese characters adapted to Japan. These originated in their initial form in the Yellow River region of China between 2000 and 1500 BC. Chinese characters can be classified into four main categories: pictorial characters (象形文字, *shōkei-moji*); indicative characters (指示文字, *shiji-moji*); compound ideographic characters (会意文字, *kaii-moji*); and phonetic-ideographic characters (形声文字, *keisei-moji*). Pictorial characters originated from pictures of objects or phe-nomena. For example:

Pictorial characters	山 *(mountain)*	川 *(river)*	木 *(tree)*	日 *(sun)*	月 *(moon)*
Pictures	〰	〰	🌳	☀	🌙

Indicative characters were created as symbolic representations of abstract concepts using points and lines. For example:

Indicative characters	一 *(one)*	二 *(two)*	三 *(three)*	上 *(above/up)*	下 *(below/down)*
Signs	—	=	≡	•̶	̶•

Compound ideographic characters were formed by combining multiple pictorial or indicative characters to bring out a new but simple idea. For example:

Compound ideographic characters	林 *(woods)*	森 *(forest)*	明 *(bright)*
Components	木 + 木 *(tree + tree)*	木 + 木 + 木 *(tree + tree + tree)*	日 + 月 *(sun + moon)*

Phonetic-ideographic characters were formed by combining an element of meaning and an ele-ment of sound. For example, the following characters all stand for some body of water:

Phonetic-ideographic characters	江 *(inlet)*	洋 *(ocean)*	河 *(river)*
Components	氵 + 工 *(water + **kō**)*	氵 + 羊 *(water + **yō**)*	氵 + 可 *(water + **ka**)*

The left side of each character, 氵, shows that the character's meaning is related to water, and the right side of each character, 工, 羊, or 可, shows how the character should be pronounced.

On-reading and kun-reading

The Japanese language is very different from the Chinese language, having distinct sounds and syllable structures in addition to its own vocabulary and grammar. When Chinese characters were adapted to Japanese as kanji, they were assigned *on*-reading (音読み, *on'yomi*) and *kun*-reading (訓読み, *kun'yomi*) pronunciations. As discussed earlier, the *on*-reading is the approximation of the Chinese pronunciation of a character and the *kun*-reading is the pronunciation of the existing native Japanese word whose meaning is similar to the given character. For example, the *on*-reading of the character 母 (mother) is *bo*, and its *kun*-reading is *haha*. In most cases, *on*-readings are used when the kanji character is a part of a kanji compound word, but *kun*-readings are used in other contexts. This can be seen in the following sentence, which reads, "My mom's mother country is America."

母の　母国　はアメリカ です 。
Haha no **bo**-koku wa　Amerika　desu

kun-reading　on-reading

Note that some kanji characters have more than one *on*-reading or *kun*-reading, and there are many exceptional readings, which will be discussed later.

Okurigana

Chinese verbs and adjectives do not require inflectional endings, but Japanese verbs and adjectives do. When a Japanese verb or adjective is written in kanji, the inflectional ending is written in kana. Such kana are called 送り仮名 *okurigana*. In modern Japanese, hiragana is used for this purpose. For example, the Japanese verb that means "to walk" has different forms; the first part (歩) is written in kanji and the rest is written in hiragana:

歩く　　　(*aruku*) walk, walks, will walk
歩いた　　(*aruita*) walked

Similarly, the Japanese adjective that means "expensive" has different forms; the first part (高) is written in kanji and the rest is written in hiragana:

高い　　　(*takai*) is expensive, are expensive
高かった　(*takakatta*) was expensive, were expensive

As you can see, a kanji character and the *okurigana* jointly represent the whole Japanese word, along with the inflectional information. *Okurigana* are also used for some adverbs (e.g., 必ず, *kanarazu*, absolutely) and nouns (e.g., 動き, *ugoki*, movement).

Furigana

Kanji characters are occasionally accompanied by kana that show how they should be read. Kana used as a pronunciation guide in this way are called *furigana* (振り仮名). These are used in newspapers for unusual readings and for characters not included in the *jōyō*-kanji discussed earlier. Japanese manga use *furigana* a lot! Elementary kanji textbooks also include *furigana*. *Furigana* are written above kanji in horizontal writing, and beside kanji in vertical writing, as shown below.

奈良公園の野生の鹿はとても人になれていて、観光客はそこで「鹿せんべい」というクラッカーを買って鹿にやります。

Horizontal Writing

奈良公園の野生の鹿はとても人になれていて、観光客はそこで「鹿せんべい」というクラッカーを買って鹿にやります。

Vertical Writing

Kanji compound words

Many words are written with a combination of two or more kanji characters. Compounds whose pronunciation is based on their *on*-reading are called Sino-Japanese compounds. These were generally created in Japan using existing kanji borrowed from Chinese. Sino-Japanese compounds constitute a large proportion of Japanese vocabulary. For example, 先生 (*sensei*, teacher) consists of two characters, 先 (ahead) and 生 (live), which are pronounced using their *on*-readings, *sen* and *sei*. The majority of Sino-Japanese compounds were created in Japan during the Meiji era (1868–1912), when Japan was being rapidly modernized. Thousands of Sino-Japanese compounds were created, as books and documents from the West were translated into Japanese. These include words such as the following:

電話 (*denwa*, telephone)
化学 (*kagaku*, chemistry)
社会 (*shakai*, society)

Many Sino-Japanese compounds created in Japan during the Meiji era were taken to China and became part of the Chinese language.

Compounds whose pronunciation is based on *kun*-readings are not called Sino-Japanese compounds, even though they are exclusively written in kanji. For example, 花見 (*hanami*, flower viewing) consists of the kanji characters 花 (flower) and 見 (look), but it is not a Sino-Japanese compound because the pronunciation is based on the *kun*-readings, *hana* and *mi* (as in *miru*).

Radicals

Most kanji characters are composed of two or more components. Each component may contribute to the kanji's meaning, sound, or merely its shape. For example, 日 is an independent kanji character meaning sun, but is also a component that lends meaning to many kanji. For example:

明 *bright*   時 *time*   晴 *clear up*

There are many kanji components, but the most basic and identifiable elements of kanji are called *radicals*. For hundreds of years, Chinese dictionaries have organized kanji characters according to their radicals. Each Chinese character was assigned a radical and placed in an appropriate section of a dictionary according to the designated radical.

Ateji

Ateji are kanji or kanji compounds that have a meaning or pronunciation unrelated to that of their source kanji. For example, the kanji compound 寿司 is an *ateji*. It was assigned to represent the Japanese word *sushi* because of its sound, ignoring the actual meaning of the kanji that constitute it. In fact, 寿 means "one's natural lifespan" and 司 means "to administer." Neither is directly related to food, but their sounds, "su" and "shi," are perfect for representing "sushi."

Another example of *ateji* is the combination of the three kanji characters 五月雨. This compound was assigned to the Japanese word *samidare* (early summer rain), because of the meanings of the kanji characters, which are "five/fifth," "month," and "rain," irrespective of their sounds. The kanji phrase 五月雨 literally means "May rain," which is perfect for representing the meaning of *samidare*. This type of *ateji* is also called *jukujikun* (熟字訓).

Ateji may occasionally be used for non-Chinese loan words. For example, 麦酒 is an *ateji* for *bīru* (beer): 麦 means "wheat" and 酒 means "liquor," so it is a perfect choice to represent "beer," although, again, it does not reflect the pronunciation of these two kanji characters. Learning *ateji* offers insight into the passion that the Japanese have for using kanji.

Kokuji

Many kanji characters were created in Japan by combining existing kanji characters, or components of a kanji character, following the basic principles of the formation of Chinese characters shown on page 8. These are called *kokuji* (国字). For example, the kanji 峠 (mountain pass) is a *kokuji*. It was created by combining three kanji characters: 山 (mountain), 上 (up), and 下 (down); it is read as *tōge*, which is the Japanese word for mountain pass. In other cases, the pronunciation of the *kokuji* is based on the *on*-reading of its main component. For example, the medical term 腺 (gland), is read as *sen* because that is the *on*-reading of the component 泉. The following are some examples of *kokuji*:

- 峠 (*tōge*, mountain pass): combination of 山 (mountain), 上 (up), and 下 (down)
- 躾 (*shitsuke*, discipline): combination of 身 (body) and 美 (beauty)
- 鰯 (*iwashi*, sardines): combination of 魚 (fish) and 弱 (weak)
- 鱈 (*tara*, codfish): combination of 魚 (fish) and 雪 (snow)
- 鯰 (*namazu*, catfish): combination of 魚 (fish) and 念 (wish)
- 腺 (*sen*, gland): combination of 月 (radical for body) and 泉 (spring)
- 膵 (*sui*, pancreas): combination of 月 (radical for body) and 萃 (collect)

Kokuji show how the Japanese people of the past made an effort to use kanji as much as possible when expressing concepts in writing.

Study tips

1. Study the book in order as each lesson and section is built upon preceding lessons and sections.
2. Listen to the audio files (link below), marked with , to learn natural Japanese pronunciation.
3. Practice reading aloud. Section C of the first nine lessons in Parts One and Two encourages you to read new characters in groups of 5, 7 and 5, like a haiku poem. New characters are introduced, randomized, then mixed with previously learned characters. First read the characters in each group, one by one, very slowly, focusing on accuracy. After you feel confident, increase your speed, and move to the next group and the next line. Pause briefly between groups, as if you were reading a haiku. Try reading the lines backward for an extra challenge.
4. At the link below you can also find printable flash cards. Try shuffling them for character-recognition practice. Also use them to find characters that look alike. For example, the hiragana わ, ね, and れ are similar, as are the hiragana も and its katakana counterpart モ. Identifying similarities and differences will help you learn characters quickly.
5. Use imagination, emotion and creative association to help you learn quickly. I like ゆ and の because they both have a nice smooth round stroke. Which ones do you like and why? The kanji section uses mnemonics to help you memorize characters—why not invent your own?
6. Learn each kanji character using words that include it, as meanings and pronunciation vary.
7. Learn the components of each kanji character. Writing 男 may seem difficult, but writing each component of it, 田 and 力, is easy!
8. Write each character ten or twenty times until your hand muscles remember it. Photocopy the blank practice sheet on page 123 for this purpose.
9. Regard handwriting as a kind of artistic expression. This makes your learning more fun!

To access the online audio recordings and printable flash cards for this book

1. Check that you have an Internet connection.
2. Type the following URL into your web browser.
   www.tuttlepublishing.com/reading-and-writing-japanese

For support, you can email us at info@tuttlepublishing.com.

PART ONE

The Hiragana Alphabet

How to learn hiragana

Hiragana is used for grammatical particles, suffixes, and inflections. It is also used for words and names in Japanese that do not have their own kanji. In this chapter, you will learn how to write all of the hiragana characters and how to use them to write words, phrases, sentences and paragraphs. Note that many of the hiragana words introduced in this section are usually written in kanji, but they are given in hiragana here for the purpose of reading and writing practice.

1. Practice writing each hiragana character stroke by stroke, in the order shown, in the blank boxes following each character.
2. Use the online audio recordings (see link on page 12) to practice pronouncing each character correctly as you learn it, as well as vocabulary words that use the character, paying attention to rhythm, beat, and pitch accent.
3. Make sure you learn to write each hiragana in the correct stroke order so you can write the character neatly and legibly.
4. Make use of the online printable flash cards to help you memorize the characters (see link on page 12).

You can reasonably master the first set of hiragana in two or three weeks. However, you can spend only three days or as long as three years! It just depends on how determined you are. I recommend you work on one lesson a day.

🎧 The 46 Basic Hiragana Characters

あ a	い i	う u	え e	お o
か ka	き ki	く ku	け ke	こ ko
さ sa	し shi	す su	せ se	そ so
た ta	ち chi	つ tsu	て te	と to
な na	に ni	ぬ nu	ね ne	の no
は ha (wa)	ひ hi	ふ fu	へ he (e)	ほ ho
ま ma	み mi	む mu	め me	も mo
や ya		ゆ yu		よ yo
ら ra	り ri	る ru	れ re	ろ ro
わ wa				を o (wo)
ん n				

🎧 The 61 Additional Hiragana Syllables

が ga	ぎ gi	ぐ gu	げ ge	ご go
ざ za	じ ji	ず zu	ぜ ze	ぞ zo
だ da	ぢ ji	づ zu	で de	ど do
ば ba	び bi	ぶ bu	べ be	ぼ bo
ぱ pa	ぴ pi	ぷ pu	ぺ pe	ぽ po

きゃ kya	きゅ kyu	きょ kyo	にゃ nya	にゅ nyu	にょ nyo
ぎゃ gya	ぎゅ gyu	ぎょ gyo	ひゃ hya	ひゅ hyu	ひょ hyo
しゃ sha	しゅ shu	しょ sho	びゃ bya	びゅ byu	びょ byo
じゃ ja	じゅ ju	じょ jo	ぴゃ pya	ぴゅ pyu	ぴょ pyo
ちゃ cha	ちゅ chu	ちょ cho	みゃ mya	みゅ myu	みょ myo
ぢゃ ja	ぢゅ ju	ぢょ jo	りゃ rya	りゅ ryu	りょ ryo

あ
い
う
え
お

Lesson 1

🎧 **A** Listen to the audio and practice saying the following five hiragana characters.

Hiragana Rōmaji Pronunciation	あ a *ah*	い i *ee*	う u *oo*	え e *eh*	お o *oh*
Example words	あさ **asa** morning	いぬ **inu** dog	うま **uma** horse	え **e** drawing	おりがみ **origami** origami

B Write the five hiragana characters, paying attention to the order and the direction of each stroke.

C Read the following random sequences of characters. Read them slowly and carefully at first, then repeat until you can read them fast. Pause between each group of five, seven and five characters so that the rhythm of each line sounds like haiku.

1. あいあいあ　　ういういあうい　　あいうあう
2. あえおえお　　おあおあいうお　　おあいうえ
3. えおあうお　　おえおいあいお　　うあえうえ

🎧 **D** Listen to the audio and practice reading and writing the following words. Once you have written the words, practice reading them again while covering the rōmaji and the English translation for an extra challenge.

1. い　i　stomach

い																		

2. お **o** tail

| お | | | | | | | | | | | | | | | | | |

3. え **e** drawings, paintings

| え | | | | | | | | | | | | | | | | | |

4. あお **ao** blue

| あ | お | | | | | | | | | | | | | | | |

5. いう **iu** to say

| い | う | | | | | | | | | | | | | | | |

6. いいえ **īe** no

| い | い | え | | | | | | | | |

7. おい **oi** nephew

| お | い | | | | | | | | | | | |

8. いい **ī** good

| い | い | | | | | | | | | | | |

9. あう **au** to meet

| あ | う | | | | | | | | | | | |

10. おおい **ōi** numerous, abundant

| お | お | い | | | | | | | | | |

🎧 **E** Listen to the audio recordings and use hiragana to write the words that you hear. Check your answers on page 124.

1. _____   2. _____   3. _____

か
き
く
け
こ

Lesson 2

🎧 **A** Listen to the audio and practice saying the following five hiragana characters.

Hiragana Rōmaji Pronunciation	か **ka** *kah*	き **ki** *kee*	く **ku** *koo*	け **ke** *keh*	こ **ko** *koh*
Example words	からて **karate** karate	きもの **kimono** kimono	くるま **kuruma** car	けむり **kemuri** smoke	こども **kodomo** child

B Write the five hiragana characters, paying attention to the order and the direction of each stroke.

フ→ カ→が	か						
ラ→ ラ→ ぎ→ き	き						
く	く						
し→ に→ け	け						
こ → こ	こ						

C Read the following random sequences of characters. Read them slowly and carefully at first, then repeat until you can read them fast. Pause between each group of five, seven and five characters so that the rhythm of each line sounds like a haiku.

1. かきかくか　　　きけきけくかき　　　けこけきけ
2. こかきこけ　　　けこかきかくき　　　こかけきく
3. あかきかき　　　うくけくおこく　　　けかきけこ

🎧 **D** Listen to the audio and practice reading and writing the following words. Once you have written the words, practice reading them again while covering the rōmaji and the English translation for an extra challenge.

1. かお　**kao**　face

か	お													

2. あき **aki** autumn

| あ | き | | | | | | | | | | | |

3. くうき **kūki** air

| く | う | き | | | | | | | | |

4. いけ **ike** pond

| い | け | | | | | | | | | | | |

5. ここ **koko** here

| こ | こ | | | | | | | | | | | |

6. こえ **koe** voice

| こ | え | | | | | | | | | | | |

7. おか **oka** hill

| お | か | | | | | | | | | | | |

8. かう **kau** to buy

| か | う | | | | | | | | | | | |

9. かく **kaku** to write

| か | く | | | | | | | | | | | |

10. おおきい **ōkī** big

| お | お | き | い | | | | | | | |

🎧 **E** Listen to the audio recordings and use hiragana to write the words that you hear. Check your answers on page 124.

I. _____   2. _____   3. _____

Lesson 3

🎧 **A** Listen to the audio and practice saying the following five hiragana characters.

Hiragana Rōmaji Pronunciation	さ **sa** *sah*	し **shi** *shee*	す **su** *soo*	せ **se** *seh*	そ **so** *soh*
Example words	さかな **sakana** fish	しま **shima** island	すし **sushi** sushi	せんせい **sensei** teacher	そら **sora** sky

B Write the five hiragana characters, paying attention to the order and the direction of each stroke.

C Read the following random sequences of characters. Read them slowly and carefully at first, then repeat until you can read them fast. Pause between each group of five, seven and five characters so that the rhythm of each line sounds like haiku.

1. ささしさし　　しすさすさすし　　すさしさし
2. せすせせそ　　そせそせそそせ　　すせそすせ
3. かさかさし　　おこそこおあそ　　こそすくせ

🎧 **D** Listen to the audio and practice reading and writing the following words. Once you have written the words, practice reading them again while covering the rōmaji and the English translation for an extra challenge.

1. くさ　**kusa**　grass

2. しか **shika** deer

し	か										

3. すし **sushi** sushi

す	し										

4. せき **seki** cough

せ	き										

5. おそい **osoi** slow

お	そ	い							

6. いし **ishi** stone

い	し										

7. きせき **kiseki** miracle

き	せ	き							

8. せかい **sekai** world

せ	か	い							

9. いす **isu** chair

い	す										

10. おかし **okashi** candy

お	か	し							

🎧 **E** Listen to the audio recordings and use hiragana to write the words that you hear. Check your answers on page 124.

1. _____   2. _____   3. _____

Lesson 4

🎧 **A** Listen to the audio and practice saying the following five hiragana characters.

Hiragana	た	ち	つ	て	と
Rōmaji	ta	chi	tsu	te	to
Pronunciation	*tah*	*chee*	*tsoo*	*teh*	*toh*
Example words	たまご	ちず	つなみ	てがみ	とら
	tamago	chizu	tsunami	tegami	tora
	egg	map	tsunami	letter	tiger

B Write the five hiragana characters, paying attention to the order and the direction of each stroke.

⹋→た→た→た	た						
⹋→ち	ち						
つ	つ						
て	て						
ヽ→と	と						

C Read the following random sequences of characters. Read them slowly and carefully at first, then repeat until you can read them fast. Pause between each group of five, seven and five characters so that the rhythm of each line sounds like haiku.

1. たちたたち　　つちつたちつて　　てとてつち
2. とてつてと　　たちてつたとた　　てとたちつ
3. さたしてつ　　さかたけてせて　　おかさえつ

🎧 **D** Listen to the audio and practice reading and writing the following words. Once you have written the words, practice reading them again while covering the rōmaji and the English translation for an extra challenge.

1. うた　**uta**　song

う	た													

2. ちかてつ **chikatetsu** subway

ち	か	て	つ								

3. くつ **kutsu** shoes

く	つ										

4. てき **teki** enemy

て	き										

5. とし **toshi** age

と	し										

6. おと **oto** sound

お	と										

7. いち **ichi** one

い	ち										

8. て **te** hand

て											

9. うち **uchi** inside, home

う	ち										

10. そと **soto** outside

そ	と										

🎧 **E** Listen to the audio recordings and use hiragana to write the words that you hear. Check your answers on page 124.

1. _____   2. _____   3. _____

Lesson 5

🎧 **A** Listen to the audio and practice saying the following five hiragana characters.

Hiragana Rōmaji Pronunciation	な **na** *nah*	に **ni** *nee*	ぬ **nu** *noo*	ね **ne** *neh*	の **no** *noh*
Example words	なまえ **namae** name	にほん **Nihon** Japan	ぬま **numa** marsh	ねこ **neko** cat	のり **nori** seaweed

B Write the five hiragana characters, paying attention to the order and the direction of each stroke.

C Read the following random sequences of characters. Read them slowly and carefully at first, then repeat until you can read them fast. Pause between each group of five, seven and five characters so that the rhythm of each line sounds like haiku.

1. なになにな   ぬねぬぬねにな   のなになぬ
2. ぬねなぬね   のなねぬねのな   なにぬねの
3. うぬすちた   けねぬないくえ   そとのにか

🎧 **D** Listen to the audio and practice reading and writing the following words. Once you have written the words, practice reading them again while covering the rōmaji and the English translation for an extra challenge.

1. なな   **nana**   seven

な	な											

2. にし **nishi** west

にし													

3. いぬ **inu** dog

いぬ													

4. ねこ **neko** cat

ねこ													

5. おの **ono** ax

おの													

6. くに **kuni** country

くに													

7. なす **nasu** eggplant

なす													

8. おかね **okane** money

おかね									

9. あな **ana** hole

あな													

10. いなか **inaka** countryside

いなか										

🎧 **E** **Listen to the audio recordings and use hiragana to write the words that you hear. Check your answers on page 124.**

1. _____   2. _____   3. _____

は
ひ
ふ
へ
ほ

Lesson 6

🎧 **A** Listen to the audio and practice saying the following five hiragana characters.

Hiragana Rōmaji Pronunciation	は **ha** *hah*	ひ **hi** *hee*	ふ **fu** *foo*	へ **he** *heh*	ほ **ho** *hoh*
Example words	はな **hana** flower	ひかり **hikari** light	ふとん **futon** futon	へや **heya** room	ほし **hoshi** star

B Write the five hiragana characters, paying attention to the order and the direction of each stroke.

C Read the following random sequences of characters. Read them slowly and carefully at first, then repeat until you can read them fast. Pause between each group of five, seven and five characters so that the rhythm of each line sounds like haiku.

1. はひはひふ   ふへほふほはひ   ほはひふへ
2. はほはほへ   ふへふふへひへ   ひふへほは
3. さはなにほ   えけへねぬのせ   なひへのへ

🎧 **D** Listen to the audio and practice reading and writing the following words. Once you have written the words, practice reading them again while covering the rōmaji and the English translation for an extra challenge.

1. はた   **hata**   flag

は	た															

2. ひと **hito** person

ひ	と											

3. ふく **fuku** clothes

ふ	く											

4. へた **heta** unskillful

へ	た											

5. ほし **hoshi** star

ほ	し											

6. はち **hachi** bee

は	ち											

7. はな **hana** flower

は	な											

8. ひ **hi** fire

ひ												

9. ひくい **hikui** low

ひ	く	い								

10. ふとい **futoi** thick

ふ	と	い								

🎧 **E** Listen to the audio recordings and use hiragana to write the words that you hear. Check your answers on page 124.

1. _____   2. _____   3. _____

Lesson 7

🎧 **A** Listen to the audio and practice saying the following five hiragana characters.

Hiragana Rōmaji Pronunciation	ま **ma** *mah*	み **mi** *mee*	む **mu** *moo*	め **me** *meh*	も **mo** *moh*
Example words	まち **machi** town	みず **mizu** water	むし **mushi** insect	めがね **megane** eyeglasses	もち **mochi** rice cake

B Write the five hiragana characters, paying attention to the order and the direction of each stroke.

C Read the following random sequences of characters. Read them slowly and carefully at first, then repeat until you can read them fast. Pause between each group of five, seven and five characters so that the rhythm of each line sounds like haiku.

1. まみまみま   むめむめめむも   もまもまめ
2. ももまもま   みめむみめまむ   まめまみむ
3. はまほまは   にけはほなたま   みなみねの

🎧 **D** Listen to the audio and practice reading and writing the following words. Once you have written the words, practice reading them again while covering the rōmaji and the English translation for an extra challenge.

1. まめ **mame** beans

ま	め												

2. みみ **mimi** ear

み	み														

3. むし **mushi** insect, bug

む	し														

4. むすこ **musuko** son

む	す	こ								

5. むすめ **musume** daughter

む	す	め								

6. め **me** eye

め															

7. もも **momo** peach

も	も														

8. あめ **ame** rain

あ	め														

9. くま **kuma** bear

く	ま														

10. かみ **kami** paper

か	み														

🎧 **E** Listen to the audio recordings and use hiragana to write the words that you hear. Check your answers on page 124.

1. _____   2. _____   3. _____

Lesson 8

🎧 **A** Listen to the audio and practice saying the following five hiragana characters.

Hiragana	や	ゆ	よ
Rōmaji	ya	yu	yo
Pronunciation	*yah*	*yoo*	*yoh*
Example words	やね	ゆめ	よる
	yane	yume	yoru
	roof	dream	night

Note These characters are also used in palatalized sounds, as will be discussed in Lesson 13.

B Write the three hiragana characters, paying attention to the order and the direction of each stroke.

C Read the following random sequences of characters. Read them slowly and carefully at first, then repeat until you can read them fast. Pause between each group of five, seven and five characters so that the rhythm of each line sounds like haiku.

1. やゆやゆよ　　　よゆやゆやゆよ　　　やよめよや
2. やまやまや　　　ゆめゆめもやむ　　　めもよはよ
3. あやまなか　　　かなゆむすゆす　　　よはなたよ

🎧 **D** Listen to the audio and practice reading and writing the following words. Once you have written the words, practice reading them again while covering the rōmaji and the English translation for an extra challenge.

1. やすい **yasui** cheap

や	す	い													

2. ゆき **yuki** snow

ゆ	き														

3. よあけ **yoake** dawn

よ	あ	け														

4. よむ **yomu** to read

よ	む														

5. おや **oya** parent

お	や														

6. つよい **tsuyoi** strong

つ	よ	い												

7. ふゆ **fuyu** winter

ふ	ゆ														

8. へや **heya** room

へ	や														

9. はなや **hanaya** flower shop

は	な	や											

10. おかゆ **okayu** rice porridge

お	か	ゆ											

🎧 **E** Listen to the audio recordings and use hiragana to write the words that you hear.
Check your answers on page 124.

1. _____   2. _____   3. _____

ら
り
る
れ
ろ

Lesson 9

🎧 **A** Listen to the audio and practice saying the following five hiragana characters.

Hiragana Rōmaji Pronunciation	ら **ra** *rah*	り **ri** *ree*	る **ru** *roo*	れ **re** *reh*	ろ **ro** *roh*
Example words	らくだ **rakuda** camel	りんご **ringo** apple	るすばん **rusuban** house-sitting	れきし **rekishi** history	ろく **roku** six

B Write the five hiragana characters, paying attention to the order and the direction of each stroke.

ⁱ↗ → ²ら	ら
¹↓ → り²	り
る	る
↓¹ → れ²	れ
²ろ	ろ

C Read the following random sequences of characters. Read them slowly and carefully at first, then repeat until you can read them fast. Pause between each group of five, seven and five characters so that the rhythm of each line sounds like haiku.

1. らりらりる   るれろらるれら   られるろり
2. るろらるろ   ゆるむやゆらよ   よろれらり
3. ちらろるさ   いりりいけいり   れねれねれ

🎧 **D** Listen to the audio and practice reading and writing the following words. Once you learn the words, practice reading them again while covering the rōmaji and the English translation for an extra challenge.

1. らく   **raku**   easy

ら	く															

2. りす **risu** squirrel

り	す											

3. ひる **hiru** noon

ひ	る											

4. これ **kore** this [one]

こ	れ											

5. てら **tera** temple

て	ら											

6. とり **tori** bird

と	り												

7. ひろい **hiroi** spacious

ひ	ろ	い					

8. こおり **kōri** ice

こ	お	り					

9. もり **mori** forest

も	り											

10. そら **sora** sky

そ	ら											

🎧 **E** Listen to the audio recordings and use hiragana to write the words that you hear. Check your answers on page 124.

I. _____   2. _____   3. _____

わ
を
ん

Lesson 10

🎧 **A** Listen to the audio and practice saying the following five hiragana characters.

Hiragana Rōmaji Pronunciation	わ **wa** *wah*	を **o (wo)** *oh*	ん **n** *n*
Example words	わた **wata** cotton		ほん **hon** book

Note 1 The hiragana を and お sound the same (**o**) in modern Japanese, but を is only used to write the direct object marker (**o**) in Japanese, and is not used in any other words.

Note 2 The hiragana ん represents a syllable-ending nasal **n** sound. It is never used at the beginning of a word. It is pronounced in the back of the mouth, and may sound like **m** or **n** depending on the syllable that follows it. ん takes one beat just by itself. By contrast, a syllable-initial nasal sound (**n** or **m**) is integrated in な, に, ぬ, ね, の, ま, み, む, め, or も.

B Write the three hiragana characters, paying attention to the order and the direction of each stroke.

🎧 **C** Listen to the audio and practice reading and writing the following words. Once you have written the words, practice reading them again while covering the rōmaji and the English translation for an extra challenge.

1. わし　**washi**　eagle

2. きをつけて　**ki o tsukete**　"Be careful!"

3. きん **kin** gold

き	ん										

4. みかん **mikan** tangerine

み	か	ん							

5. うんてん **unten** driving

う	ん	て	ん						

🎧 **D** Listen to the audio recordings and use hiragana to write the words that you hear. Check your answers on page 124.

1. _____   2. _____   3. _____

🎧 **E** Practice reading the hiragana characters as shown in this table as smoothly as possible. Start by reading the top line from left to right and work your way down the chart until you can memorize the order: あ い う え お か き く け こ, etc. This is the "alphabet" order used in Japanese dictionaries, so it's useful to know.

あ	い	う	え	お	
か	き	く	け	こ	
さ	し	す	せ	そ	
た	ち	つ	て	と	
な	に	ぬ	ね	の	
は	ひ	ふ	へ	ほ	
ま	み	む	め	も	
や		ゆ		よ	
ら	り	る	れ	ろ	
わ				を	ん

Lesson 11 Voicing mark (゛) and p-mark (゜)

There are two diacritical marks that can be placed at the upper right corner of a kana character. One is the voicing mark (゛), called *dakuten* (濁点) in Japanese. This makes the initial consonant in **k-**, **s-**, **t-**, or **h-** syllables voiced. For example, **k**-syllables become g-syllables:

か	(ka)	becomes	が	(ga)
き	(ki)	becomes	ぎ	(gi)
く	(ku)	becomes	ぐ	(gu)
け	(ke)	becomes	げ	(ge)
こ	(ko)	becomes	ご	(go)

The main difference between the unvoiced consonants **k**, **s**, **t**, and **h** and their voiced equivalents **g**, **z**, **d** and **b** is the vibration of your vocal cords. Touch your neck near your Adam's apple and say **k** and **g**. You'll feel a vibration when saying **g**, but not when saying **k**.

The other diacritical mark is the **p**-mark (゜), called *handakuten* (半濁点) in Japanese. This mark is used only with the **h**-syllables and it changes them to **p**-syllables:

は	(ha)	becomes	ぱ	(pa)
ひ	(hi)	becomes	ぴ	(pi)
ふ	(fu)	becomes	ぷ	(pu)
へ	(he)	becomes	ぺ	(pe)
ほ	(ho)	becomes	ぽ	(po)

🎧 **A** The following are all the hiragana characters that have either the voicing mark or the p-mark. Listen to the audio and practice pronouncing them.

1.	が	ga	ぎ	gi	ぐ	gu	げ	ge	ご	go
2.	ざ	za	じ	ji	ず	zu	ぜ	ze	ぞ	zo
3.	だ	da	ぢ	ji	づ	zu	で	de	ど	do
4.	ば	ba	び	bi	ぶ	bu	べ	be	ぼ	bo
5.	ぱ	pa	ぴ	pi	ぷ	pu	ぺ	pe	ぽ	po

Note じ and ち both sound like **ji**, and ず and づ both sound like **zu**. The sound **ji** is represented by じ in most words, but by ぢ in certain words such as はなぢ (*hana-ji*, nosebleed) and ちぢむ (*chijimu*, to shrink). Similarly, the sound **zu** is usually represented by ず in most words, but by づ in some words such as みかづき (*mika-zuki*, crescent moon) and つづく (*tsuzuku*, to continue).

🎧 **B** Read the following pairs of words, paying attention to voicing. Then check your pronunciation using the audio recordings.

1.	かき	persimmon	かぎ	key
2.	きん	gold	ぎん	silver
3.	し	poem	じ	characters, scripts
4.	かがく	chemistry	ががく	ancient Japanese court music
5.	こま	top (toy)	ごま	sesame
6.	はら	belly	ばら	rose

🎧 **C** Listen to the audio and practice pronouncing and writing the following words. For a greater challenge, cover the rōmaji and the English translation and write each word down as you hear it.

1. てんぷら **tenpura** tempura

て	ん	ぷ	ら						

2. えんぴつ **enpitsu** pencil

え	ん	ぴ	つ						

3. かんぺき **kanpeki** perfect

か	ん	ぺ	き						

4. うなぎ **unagi** eel

う	な	ぎ						

5. おりがみ **origami** origami

お	り	が	み					

6. しごと **shigoto** job, work

し	ご	と						

7. べんごし **bengoshi** lawyer

べ	ん	ご	し					

8. およぐ **oyogu** to swim

お	よ	ぐ						

🎧 **D** Listen to the audio recordings and use hiragana to write the words that you hear. Check your answers on page 124.

1. .... 3. .... 5. ....

2. .... 4. .... 6. ....

Lesson 12 Long vowels and double consonants

LONG VOWELS

The five basic Japanese vowels (**a**, **i**, **u**, **e**, and **o**) have lengthened counterparts (**ā**, **ī**, **ū**, **ē**, and **ō**) Long vowels are written by adding あ、い、う、え, or お to the syllable. Compare と (**to**, door) and とお (**tō**, ten).

Note 1 A long **ō** sound is usually written with う in hiragana, as in the word ありがとう (**arigatō** thanks).

Note 2 A long **ē** sound is usually written **ei** in Japanese, both in hiragana and rōmaji, as in the word えいご (**eigo**, English).

🎧 **A** Read the following pairs of words, paying attention to the length of the vowels. Then check your pronunciation using the audio recordings.

1.	とり	bird	とおり	street
2.	ふけい	patents	ふうけい	scenery
3.	ゆめ	dream	ゆうめい	famous
4.	おばさん	aunt	おばあさん	grandmother
5.	おじさん	uncle	おじいさん	grandfather

🎧 **B** Listen to the audio and practice pronouncing and writing the following words. For a greater challenge, cover the rōmaji and the English translation and write each word down as you hear it.

1. おかあさん **okāsan** mother

お	か	あ	さ	ん									

2. おとうさん **otōsan** father

お	と	う	さ	ん									

3. おにいさん **onīsan** older brother

お	に	い	さ	ん									

4. おねえさん **onēsan** older sister

お	ね	え	さ	ん									

5. せんせい **sensei** teacher

せ	ん	せ	い										

6. がくせい **gakusei** student

が	く	せ	い										

DOUBLE CONSONANTS

Japanese has some double consonants, such as **kk**, **ss**, **tt** and **pp**, which are pronounced as single consonants preceded by a brief pause. That pause is represented by the small-sized hiragana character っ, as in きって (**kitte**, postage stamp). See page 45 for the positioning of っ.

🎧 **C** Read the following pairs of words. Then check your pronunciation using the audio recordings.

1.	さか	hill	さっか	writer
2.	おと	sound	おっと	husband
3.	かき	persimmon	かっき	liveliness
4.	みつ	honey	みっつ	three pieces
5.	にほん	Japan	にっぽん	Japan

🎧 **D** Listen to the audio and practice pronouncing and writing the following words. For a greater challenge, cover the rōmaji and the English translation and write each word down as you hear it.

1. きって **kitte** postage stamp

き	っ	て							

2. まっすぐ **massugu** straight

ま	っ	す	ぐ						

3. きっぷ **kippu** ticket

き	っ	ぷ							

4. がっこう **gakkō** school

が	っ	こ	う						

5. ざっし **zasshi** magazine

ざ	っ	し							

6. はっぱ **happa** leaf

は	っ	ぱ							

🎧 **E** Listen to the audio recordings and use hiragana to write the words that you hear. Check your answers on page 124.

1. _____   3. _____   5. _____

2. _____   4. _____   6. _____

Lesson 13 Palatalized sounds

A Japanese syllable may begin with a palatalized consonant—a consonant to which a **y**-like sound is added. Such syllables, called **yōon** (拗音) in Japanese, are written by combining two kana characters: one that includes the initial consonant plus the vowel **i**, and a small-sized **ya** や, **yu** ゆ, or **yo** よ. For example, the syllable **kya** is written as きゃ.

🎧 **A** Listen to the audio and practice pronouncing the following palatalized syllables.

1.	きゃ **kya**	きゅ **kyu**	きょ **kyo**
2.	ぎゃ **gya**	ぎゅ **gyu**	ぎょ **gyo**
3.	しゃ **sha**	しゅ **shu**	しょ **sho**
4.	じゃ **ja**	じゅ **ju**	じょ **jo**
5.	ちゃ **cha**	ちゅ **chu**	ちょ **cho**
6.	ぢゃ **ja**	ぢゅ **ju**	ぢょ **jo**
7.	にゃ **nya**	にゅ **nyu**	にょ **nyo**
8.	ひゃ **hya**	ひゅ **hyu**	ひょ **hyo**
9.	びゃ **bya**	びゅ **byu**	びょ **byo**
10.	ぴゃ **pya**	ぴゅ **pyu**	ぴょ **pyo**
11.	みゃ **mya**	みゅ **myu**	みょ **myo**
12.	りゃ **rya**	りゅ **ryu**	りょ **ryo**

🎧 **B** Read the following pairs of words. Then check your pronunciation using the audio recordings. No need to pay too much attention to word meanings for this exercise, because the focus here is on the palatalized sounds.

1.	がく	(picture) frame	ぎゃく	opposite
2.	まく	membrane	みゃく	pulse
3.	すうじ	numbers	しゅうじ	penmanship, calligraphy
4.	つうか	passing	ちゅうか	Chinese-style
5.	ろう	wax	りょう	dormitory
6.	ほうしき	formula, method	ひょうしき	sign, mark
7.	らく	easy	りゃく	abbreviation

🎧 **C** Listen to the pronunciation of the following words using the audio recordings and practice pronouncing and writing them. For a greater challenge, cover the rōmaji and the English translation and write down the words as you hear them.

1. とうきょう **Tōkyō** Tokyo

と	う	き	ょ	う					

2. じゅうどう **jūdō** judo

じ	ゅ	う	ど	う					

3. ひゃく **hyaku** hundred

ひ	ゃ	く							

4. りゅう **ryū** dragon

り	ゅ	う							

5. りょうり **ryōri** cooking

り	ょ	う	り				

6. ぎゅうにゅう **gyūnyū** milk

ぎ	ゅ	う	に	ゅ	う		

7. きょういく **kyōiku** education

き	ょ	う	い	く			

8. しゃかい **shakai** society

し	ゃ	か	い				

9. しゅうまつ **shūmatsu** weekend

し	ゅ	う	ま	つ			

10. おもちゃ **omocha** toy

お	も	ち	ゃ				

11. ちょっと **chotto** a little bit

ち	ょ	っ	と				

12. にんぎょう **ningyō** doll

に	ん	ぎ	ょ	う			

🎧 **D** Listen to the audio recordings and use hiragana to write the words that you hear. Check your answers on page 124.

1. ....

2. ....

3. ....

4. ....

5. ....

6. ....

Lesson 14 Reading and writing basic words

Now you can read any words written in hiragana!

A The following are basic Japanese words. Read them aloud by yourself, then listen to the audio to see if you pronounced each one correctly. For a greater challenge, cover the hiragana and write each word down as you hear it.

🎧 1. Food categories

くだもの	fruit
さかな	fish
にく	meat
やさい	vegetable

🎧 2. Colors

あか	red
あお	blue
しろ	white
くろ	black
きいろ	yellow

🎧 3. Animals

いぬ	dog
ねこ	cat
さる	monkey
ぞう	elephant
ぶた	pig

🎧 4. Actions

いく	to go
たべる	to eat
のむ	to drink
かう	to buy
かく	to write
ねる	to sleep

🎧 5. Sports

からて	karate
じゅうどう	judo
けんどう	kendo
たっきゅう	table tennis
やきゅう	baseball

🎧 6. Weather

さむい	cold
あつい	hot
すずしい	cool
あたたかい	warm
あめ	rain
ゆき	snow
たいふう	typhoon

B Listen to the audio recording and use hiragana to write the words that you hear for each part of the body in the illustration. Check your answers on page 124.

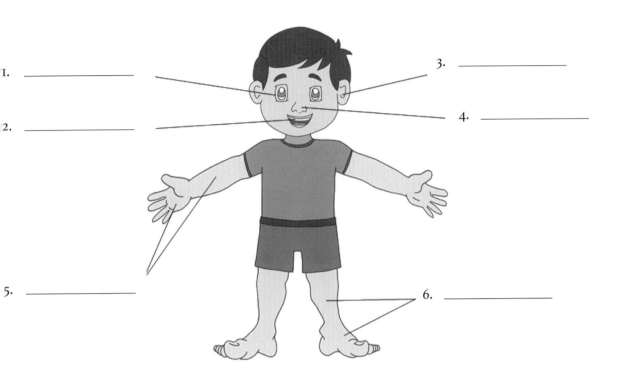

1. _____

2. _____

3. _____

4. _____

5. _____

6. _____

Lesson 15 Writing sentences and paragraphs

There are some writing conventions that must be observed when writing sentences and paragraphs in Japanese.

1. は, へ, AND を

The topic marker **wa** and the direction marker **e** are written with は and へ, respectively. In addition, remember to use を, instead of お, to represent the direct-object marker **o**.

2. PUNCTUATION

No space is needed between words in Japanese writing. In formal writing, no question marks or exclamation points are used, although the Western "?" and "!" are often used in casual writing and some published novels.

A small circle (。) called a *kuten* (句点) is placed at the end of each sentence. A short stroke (、) called a *tōten* (読点) is placed after long phrases or other places that would be helpful for readers. Unlike the comma in English, there is no strict rule on when and where the *tōten* should be placed in Japanese. Quoted speech is indicated by the opening quotation mark 「 and the closing quotaton mark 」. You can see these punctuation marks in the sentences below:

すみません。 I'm sorry.
だいじょうぶですか。 Are you all right?
はい、そうです。 Yes, that's right.
やまださんは「こんにちは。」と、いいました。 "Hello," said Ms. Yamada.

A fat dot (・) called a *nakaten* (中点) is used to separate words in a line. It is also placed between given and family names rendered in katakana.

アガサ・クリスティー   Agatha Christie
ジョン・アーンスト・スタインベック   John Ernst Steinbeck

3. TEXT DIRECTION

Japanese paragraphs are written either horizontally from left to right, as in English, or vertically from top to bottom and from right to left on a page. In modern Japanese, literary texts are generally written vertically from right to left, but other types of texts, such as business documents, contracts, academic or research papers and books, instruction manuals and memos are conventionally written horizontally from left to right.

The start of a paragraph is marked by an indentation the size of one kana character. A line break may occur before any character, even within a word, but not before a *kuten*, a *tōten*, or a closing quotation mark. Pay attention to the position and the direction of *kuten*, *tōten*, small characters, elongation marks in katakana (see page 47), punctuation marks and quotation marks. They are placed differently depending on whether the writing is horizontal or vertical, as you can see in the following excerpt of a letter from Akiko Suzuki to Keiko Yamada (you can find the rōmaji and English translation on page 125):

さむくなりましたが、山田さん
はお元気ですか。こちらは皆、元
気にしています。花子は今、高校
生です。「早く大学に入学した
い。」と、言っています。毎日フ
ルートとクラリネットのれん
しゅうをしています。　　　… →

Horizontal writing

す。…↓

さむくなりましたが、山田さんはお元気
ですか。こちらは皆、元気にしています。
花子は今、高校生です。「早く大学に入学
したい。」と、言っています。毎日フルー
トとクラリネットのれんしゅうをしていま

Vertical writing

In typed texts, the small **tsu** つ (see page 39) and the small **ya** や, **yu** ゅ, or **yo** ょ (see page 40), take the lower half of the space in horizontal writing, but the right half of the space in vertical writing, as you can see above. On traditional squared composition paper called *genkō yōshi* (原稿用紙), the quadrant in which these small-sized characters are placed depends on whether the text is written horizontally or vertically, as shown below:

Horizontal writing

Vertical writing

🎧 **A** The following is a personal introduction written by a Japanese student called Junko Mori (in Japanese, names are usually given in the order family name followed by first name). Read it through, then listen to the audio recording to see if you read it correctly. Rōmaji and English text can be found on page 125.

はじめまして。わたしのなまえはもりじゅんこです。よろしく
おねがいします。

Vocabulary

はじめまして。	How do you do.
わたし	I / me
わたしの	my
なまえ	name
は	topic marker (pronounced "**wa**")
です	is / are
よろしくおねがいします。	Pleased to meet you.

B Copy Junko's personal introduction vertically and horizontally in the boxes below.

PART TWO

The Katakana Alphabet

How to learn katakana

Katakana is mainly used to represent words and names from non-Chinese foreign culture. In this chapter you will learn to write all the katakana characters and how to use them.

1. Practice writing each katakana character stroke by stroke, in the order shown, in the blank boxes following each character.
2. Use the online audio recordings to practice pronouncing each katakana character correctly as you learn it, as well as vocabulary words that use the character, paying attention to rhythm, beat, and pitch accent. Make use of the online printable flash cards to help you memorize the characters. You can find the link for online recordings and downloadable flash cards on page 12.
3. Make sure you learn to write each katakana in the correct stroke order so you can write the character neatly and legibly.
4. Rules for voicing marks, double consonants and palatalized sounds are the same as for hiragana, and are not repeated here. But there are two conventions that are unique to katakana:
   (i) Long vowels are represented by the elongation mark ー, rather than by an additional character as in hiragana. This mark is a horizontal bar if you are writing horizontally, but a vertical bar if you are writing vertically.
   (ii) The character ウ (**U**) can be written with a voicing mark (ヴ) to approximate the foreign sound "v." You can see examples of this usage on page 71.

🎧 The 46 Basic Katakana Characters

ア a	イ i	ウ u	エ e	オ o
カ ka	キ ki	ク ku	ケ ke	コ ko
サ sa	シ shi	ス su	セ se	ソ so
タ ta	チ chi	ツ tsu	テ te	ト to
ナ na	ニ ni	ヌ nu	ネ ne	ノ no
ハ ha (wa)	ヒ hi	フ fu	ヘ he (e)	ホ ho
マ ma	ミ mi	ム mu	メ me	モ mo
ヤ ya		ユ yu		ヨ yo
ラ ra	リ ri	ル ru	レ re	ロ ro
ワ wa				ヲ o (wo)
ン n				

🎧 Additional Katakana Syllables

ガ ga	ギ gi	グ gu	ゲ ge	ゴ go
ザ za	ジ ji	ズ zu	ゼ ze	ゾ zo
ダ da	ヂ ji	ヅ zu	デ de	ド do
バ ba	ビ bi	ブ bu	ベ be	ボ bo
パ pa	ピ pi	プ pu	ペ pe	ポ po

キャ kya	キュ kyu	キョ kyo		ニャ nya	ニュ nyu	ニョ nyo
ギャ gya	ギュ gyu	ギョ gyo		ヒャ hya	ヒュ hyu	ヒョ hyo
シャ sha	シュ shu	ショ sho		ビャ bya	ビュ byu	ビョ byo
ジャ ja	ジュ ju	ジョ jo		ピャ pya	ピュ pyu	ピョ pyo
チャ cha	チュ chu	チョ cho		ミャ mya	ミュ myu	ミョ myo
ヂャ ja	ヂュ ju	ヂョ jo		リャ rya	リュ ryu	リョ ryo

ア
イ
ウ
エ
オ

Lesson 16

🎧 **A** Listen to the audio and practice saying the following five katakana characters.

Katakana	ア	イ	ウ	エ	オ
Hiragana	あ	い	う	え	お
Example words	アパート	イラスト	ウール	エンジン	オムレツ
	apartment	illustration	wool	engine	omelet

B Write the five katakana characters, paying attention to the order and the direction of each stroke.

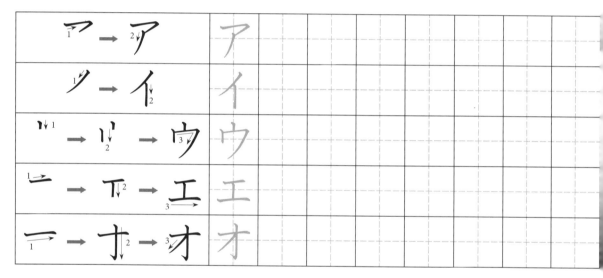

C Practice reading the following random sequences of characters. Pay attention to the elongation mark ⌐ that shows long vowels!

1. アイアウイ　　　イウイエウエウ　　　エオエオア
2. アオアオイ　　　ウエウエウーエ　　　イーエアオ

🎧 **D** Write the missing katakana character(s) in each word, then practice pronunciation by listening to the audio recording.

1. アイス　　**aisu**　ice cream

ア	イ	ス		ス		ス		ス		ス		ス

2. アプリ　　**apuri**　app

ア	プ	リ		プ	リ		プ	リ		プ	リ		プ	リ		プ	リ

50 *PART TWO: THE KATAKANA ALPHABET*

3. アレルギー **arerugī** allergy

| ア | レ | ル | ギ | ー | | レ | ル | ギ | ー | | レ | ル | ギ | ー | | レ | ル | ギ | ー |

4. インターネット **intānetto** Internet

| イ | ン | タ | ー | ネ | ッ | ト | | ン | タ | ー | ネ | ッ | ト |

5. ウクレレ **ukurere** ukulele

| ウ | ク | レ | レ | | ク | レ | レ | | ク | レ | レ | | ク | レ | レ | | ク | レ | レ |

6. エネルギー **enerugī** energy

| エ | ネ | ル | ギ | ー | | ネ | ル | ギ | ー | | ネ | ル | ギ | ー | | ネ | ル | ギ | ー |

7. オートバイ **ōtobai** motorcycle

| オ | ー | ト | バ | イ | | ー | ト | バ | | ー | ト | バ | | ー | ト | バ |

8. オアシス **oashisu** oasis

| オ | ア | シ | ス | | シ | ス | | シ | ス | | シ | ス | | シ | ス |

9. エアコン **eakon** air-conditioning

| エ | ア | コ | ン | | コ | ン | | コ | ン | | コ | ン | | コ | ン |

10. オイル **oiru** oil

| オ | イ | ル | | ル | | ル | | ル | | ル | | ル |

11. ウイルス **uirusu** virus

| ウ | イ | ル | ス | | ル | ス | | ル | ス | | ル | ス | | ル | ス |

🎧 **E** Listen to the audio and fill each of the blanks with a katakana character. You can find the answers on page 125.

1. | | | ロ | ン |

2. | | プ | ロ | ン |

3. | | ー | ブ | ン |

Lesson 17

🎧 **A** Listen to the audio and practice saying the following five katakana characters.

Katakana	カ	キ	ク	ケ	コ
Hiragana	か	き	く	け	こ
Example words	カレー curry	キッチン kitchen	クラス class	ケープ cape	コーヒー coffee

B Write the five katakana characters, paying attention to the order and the direction of each stroke.

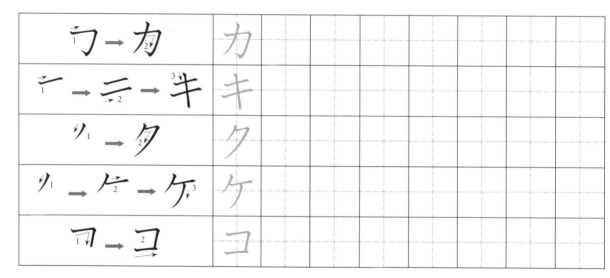

C Practice reading the following random sequences of characters. Pay attention to the voicing mark ゛, which is used the same way as in hiragana (see page 36).

1. カキカクカ   キケキケクーキ   ケコケキケ
2. コカガキギ   ケコカキカクグ   コゴカーケク
3. アカキカキ   ウクケゲオコク   ケカキケコ

🎧 **D** Write the missing katakana character(s) in each word, then practice pronunciation by listening to the audio recording.

1. カジノ   **kajino**   casino

カ	ジ	ノ	ジ	ノ	ジ	ノ	ジ	ノ	ジ	ノ	ジ	ノ

2. ガソリン   **gasorin**   gasoline

ガ	ソ	リ	ン	ソ	リ	ン	ソ	リ	ン	ソ	リ	ン	ソ	リ	ン

3. キーボード **kībōdo** keyboard

| キ | ー | ボ | ー | ド | | | ボ | ー | ド | | | ボ | ー | ド | | | ボ | ー | ド |

4. ギター **gitā** guitar

| ギ | タ | ー | | タ | ー | | タ | ー | | タ | ー | | タ | ー | | タ | ー |

5. クレヨン **kureyon** crayon

| ク | レ | ヨ | ン | | レ | ヨ | ン | | レ | ヨ | ン | | レ | ヨ | ン | | レ | ヨ | ン |

6. ケース **kēsu** case

| ケ | ー | ス | | | ス | | | ス | | | ス | | | ス | | | ス |

7. ゲーム **gēmu** game

| ゲ | ー | ム | | | ム | | | ム | | | ム | | | ム | | | ム |

8. ココア **kokoa** cocoa

| コ | コ | ア | | | | | | | | | | | | | | | | | |

9. キウイ **kiui** kiwi fruit

| キ | ウ | イ | | | | | | | | | | | | | | | | | |

10. グラフ **gurafu** graph

| グ | ラ | フ | | ラ | フ | | ラ | フ | | ラ | フ | | ラ | フ | | ラ | フ |

11. ゴルフ **gorufu** golf

| ゴ | ル | フ | | ル | フ | | ル | フ | | ル | フ | | ル | フ | | ル | フ |

🎧 **E** Listen to the audio and fill each of the blanks with a katakana character. You can find the answers on page 125.

1. | | ラ |

2. | | メ | ラ |

3. | | ー |

Lesson 18

🎧 **A** Listen to the audio and practice saying the following five katakana characters.

Katakana	サ	シ	ス	セ	ソ
Hiragana	さ	し	す	せ	そ
Example words	サービス service	シチュー stew	スーツ suit	セメント cement	ソファー sofa

B Write the five katakana characters, paying attention to the order and the direction of each stroke.

一 → 十 → サ	サ						
丶 → 丷 → シ	シ						
ヲ → ス	ス						
フ → セ	セ						
丶 → ソ	ソ						

C Practice reading the following random sequences of characters.

1. サザシサシ　　　ジスサスサスシ　　　ズサシサシ
2. セスセゼソ　　　ソセゾセソーゼ　　　スセソズセ
3. カサアガシ　　　キシエスケーゼ　　　コソスクセ

🎧 **D** Write the missing katakana character(s) in each word, then practice pronunciation by listening to the audio recording.

1. サッカー　**sakkā**　soccer

サ	ッ	カ	ー			ッ			ッ			ッ			ッ

2. シール　**shīru**　sticker

シ	ー	ル			ル		ル		ル		ル		ル

3. スーパー　**sūpā**　supermarket

スーパー		パー		パー		パー		パー

4. セレブ　**serebu**　celebrity

セレブ	レブ	レブ	レブ	レブ	レブ

5. ソプラノ　**sopurano**　soprano

ソプラノ	プラノ	プラノ	プラノ	プラノ

🎧 **E** Listen to the audio and practice reading and writing the following words.

1. サイズ　**saizu**　size

サイズ				

2. スキー　**sukī**　skiing

スキー				

3. ソーセージ　**sōsēji**　sausage

ソーセージ				

4. ソース　**sōsu**　sauce

ソース				

5. シーソー　**shīsō**　seesaw

シーソー				

🎧 **F** Listen to the audio and fill each of the blanks with a katakana character. You can find the answers on page 125.

1. | | ン | ラ |
|---|---|---|

2. | | | フ |
|---|---|---|

3. | | | ー |
|---|---|---|

Lesson 19

A Listen to the audio and practice saying the following five katakana characters.

Katakana	タ	チ	ツ	テ	ト
Hiragana	た	ち	つ	て	と
Example words	タクシー taxi	チーム team	ツリー tree	テニス tennis	トラック truck

B Write the five katakana characters, paying attention to the order and the direction of each stroke.

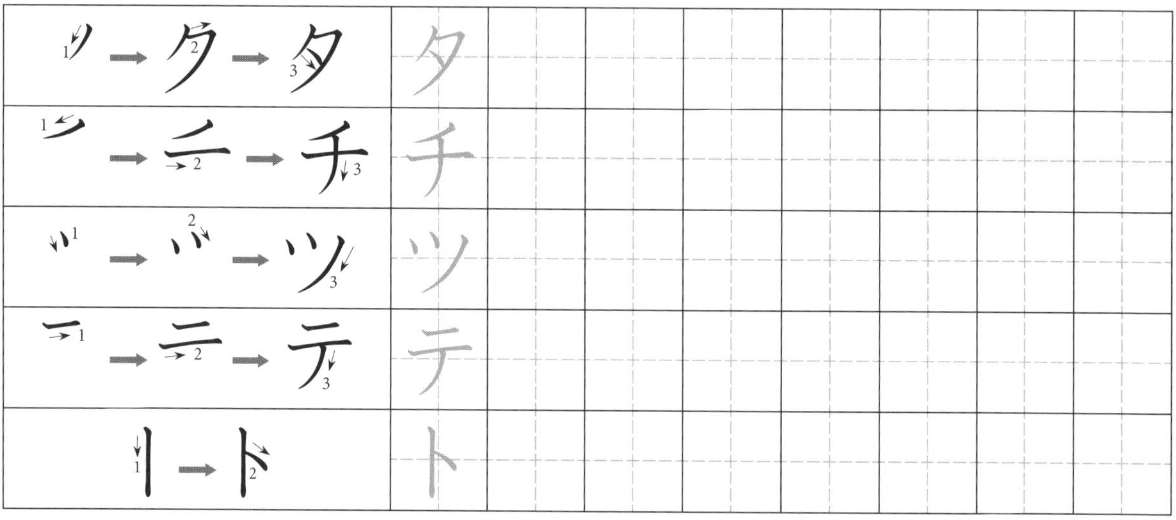

C Practice reading the following random sequences of characters. Pay attention to the double consonants, which come after the small ッ! See page 39 for a reminder.

1. タチタダチ　　ツチツヅチツテ　　テトテツデ
2. トテツットト　　タチテトタッタ　　テトタッタ
3. ウサズテデ　　トテツタデータ　　チドキック

D Read the following words. Then use the audio to check your pronunciation.

1. タイツ　tights
2. チーター　cheetah
3. ツイード　tweed
4. テスト　test
5. ドイツ　Germany

🎧 **E** Listen to the audio and practice reading and writing the following words. For a greater challenge, cover the rōmaji and the English translation.

1. ダイエット **daietto** diet

ダ	イ	エ	ッ	ト										

2. チーズ **chīzu** cheese

チ	ー	ズ									

3. ツアー **tsuā** tour

ツ	ア	ー									

4. デート **dēto** date

デ	ー	ト									

5. ドア **doa** door

ド	ア												

6. ターゲット **tāgetto** target

タ	ー	ゲ	ッ	ト										

7. トースター **tōsutā** toaster

ト	ー	ス	タ	ー										

8. コート **kōto** coat

コ	ー	ト											

🎧 **F** Listen to the audio and fill each of the blanks with a katakana character. You can find the answers on page 125.

1.

		ヤ

2.

3.

	レ	ビ

ナ
ニ
ヌ
ネ
ノ

Lesson 20

🎧 **A** Listen to the audio and practice saying the following five katakana characters.

Katakana	ナ	ニ	ヌ	ネ	ノ
Hiragana	な	に	ぬ	ね	の
Example words	ナプキン napkin	ニット knitwear	ヌードル noodle	ネオン neon	ノルマ quota

B Write the five katakana characters, paying attention to the order and the direction of each stroke.

一 → ナ	ナ							
一 → ニ	ニ							
フ → ヌ	ヌ							
→ ラ → ネ → ネ	ネ							
ノ	ノ							

C Practice reading the following random sequences of characters.

1. ナニナニナ   ヌネヌヌネニナ   ノナニナヌ
2. ヌネナーネ   ノナネヌネノナ   ナニヌーネ
3. イダナニト   ケネットイグセ   ノナカザニ

🎧 **D** Read the following words. Then use the audio to check your pronunciation.

1. ナッツ   nuts
2. ニーズ   needs
3. ヌード   nude
4. ネクター   nectar (drink)
5. ノイズ   noise

🎧 **E** Listen to the audio and practice reading and writing the following words. For a greater challenge, cover the rōmaji and the English translation.

1. ナース　**nāsu**　nurse

ナ	ー	ス									

2. ニス　**nisu**　varnish (coating)

ニ	ス											

3. カヌー　**kanū**　canoe

カ	ヌ	ー						

4. ネット　**netto**　Internet

ネ	ッ	ト						

5. ノート　**nōto**　notebook

ノ	ー	ト						

6. ケニア　**Kenia**　Kenya

ケ	ニ	ア						

7. テニス　**tenisu**　tennis

テ	ニ	ス						

🎧 **F** Listen to the audio and fill each of the blanks with a katakana character. You can find the answers on page 125.

1.
	フ

2.

3.
		レ

Lesson 21

🎧 **A** Listen to the audio and practice saying the following five katakana characters.

Katakana	ハ	ヒ	フ	ヘ	ホ
Hiragana	は	ひ	ふ	へ	ほ
Example words	ハム ham	ヒント hint	フルーツ fruit	ヘリコプター helicopter	ホテル hotel

B Write the five katakana characters, paying attention to the order and the direction of each stroke.

ノ → ハ	ハ					
ー → ヒ	ヒ					
フ	フ					
ヘ	ヘ					
ー → ナ → オ → ホ	ホ					

C Practice reading the following random sequences of characters. Pay attention to the p-mark, which works in the same way as for hiragana (see page 36).

1. ハヒハヒフ   フヘホフホハヒ   ホハヒフヘ
2. ハバパハバ   フブプペベプペ   ピポボビボ
3. ニクッツタ   ピノプセコノビ   ヌネポッポ

🎧 **D** Read the following words. Then use the audio to check your pronunciation.

1. バター   butter
2. ピザ   pizza
3. フック   hook
4. ベッド   bed
5. ポケット   pocket

🎧 **E** Listen to the audio and practice reading and writing the following words. For a greater challenge, cover the rōmaji and the English translation.

1. バス　**basu**　bus

バ	ス											

2. ビーフ　**bīfu**　beef

ビ	ー	フ						

3. ブーツ　**būtsu**　boots

ブ	ー	ツ						

4. ペット　**petto**　pet

ペ	ッ	ト						

5. ポーク　**pōku**　pork

ポ	ー	ク						

6. コップ　**koppu**　tumbler

コ	ッ	プ						

7. バナナ　**banana**　banana

バ	ナ	ナ						

8. コーヒー　**kōhī**　coffee

コ	ー	ヒ	ー								

🎧 **F** Listen to the audio and fill each of the blanks with a katakana character. You can find the answers on page 125.

1. | | ン | | | |
|---|---|---|---|---|

2. | | | | |
|---|---|---|---|

3. | | ル | ン |
|---|---|---|

Lesson 22

🎧 **A** Listen to the audio and practice saying the following five katakana characters.

Katakana	マ	ミ	ム	メ	モ
Hiragana	ま	み	む	め	も
Example words	マカロニ macaroni	ミント mint	ムース moose	メニュー menu	モデル model

B Write the five katakana characters, paying attention to the order and the direction of each stroke.

1.ワ → 2.マ	マ							
1.ゝ → 2.ミ → 3.ミ	ミ							
ム1 → ム2	ム							
1.ノ → 2.メ	メ							
モ1 → モ2 → モ3	モ							

C Practice reading the following random sequences of characters.

1. マミマミマ　　　ムメムメメムモ　　　モマモマメ
2. モアマーマ　　　ミメナメミマム　　　マメマミム
3. パマホマバ　　　ゲミフムピット　　　ヘホメーヌ

🎧 **D** Read the following words. Then use the audio to check your pronunciation.

1. マット　　　　mat
2. ミット　　　　mitt
3. ハム　　　　　ham
4. メイド　　　　maid
5. モップ　　　　mop

🎧 **E** Listen to the audio and practice reading and writing the following words. For a greater challenge, cover the rōmaji and the English translation.

1. マスク　**masuku**　(face) mask

マ	ス	ク								

2. ミートソース　**mītosōsu**　meat sauce

ミ	ー	ト	ソ	ー	ス				

3. ムード　**mūdo**　mood

ム	ー	ド								

4. メイク　**meiku**　makeup

メ	イ	ク								

5. モザイク　**mozaiku**　mosaic

モ	ザ	イ	ク									

6. ホームシック　**hōmushikku**　homesick

ホ	ー	ム	シ	ッ	ク						

7. モーター　**mōtā**　motor

モ	ー	タ	ー									

8. ミッキーマウス　**mikkīmausu**　Mickey Mouse

ミ	ッ	キ	ー	マ	ウ	ス						

🎧 **F** Listen to the audio and fill each of the blanks with a katakana character. You can find the answers on page 125.

1.

	ロ	ン

2.

		ロ		

3.

ヤ
ユ
ヨ

Lesson 23

🎧 **A** Listen to the audio and practice saying the following five katakana characters.

Katakana	ヤ	ユ	ヨ
Hiragana	や	ゆ	よ
Example words	ヤンキー delinquent	ユートピア utopia	ヨーロッパ Europe

B Write the five katakana characters paying attention to the order and the direction of each stroke.

⁷→²ヤ ヤ							
⁷→²ユ ユ							
⁷→⁷→³ヨ ヨ							

C Practice reading the following random sequences of characters. Pay attention to the palatalized sounds (small ャ, ュ, or ョ)! See page 40 for a reminder of how these work.

1. ヤユヤユヨ   ヨユヤユヤユヨ   ヤヨユヨヤ
2. ヤマヤマヤ   ユメユメモヤム   メモヨマヨ
3. シャカヤマナ   キョガカナムース   チュマコップ

🎧 **D** Read the following words. Then use the audio to check your pronunciation. For a greater challenge, cover the English translation. Pay special attention to the size of the characters in this exercise.

1. ヤード   yard (unit of length)
2. ユニーク   unique
3. ユニセフ   UNICEF
4. コヨーテ   coyote
5. ニューヨーク   New York

🎧 **E** Listen to the audio and practice reading and writing the following words. For a greater challenge, cover the rōmaji and the English translation. Pay special attention to the size of the characters in this exercise.

1. ミュージック　**mūjikku**　music

ミ	ュ	ー	ジ	ッ	ク										

2. ジュース　**jūsu**　juice

ジ	ュ	ー	ス												

3. ユーモア　**yūmoa**　humor

ユ	ー	モ	ア												

4. マヨネーズ　**mayonēzu**　mayonnaise

マ	ヨ	ネ	ー	ズ								

5. ケチャップ　**kechappu**　ketchup

ケ	チ	ャ	ッ	プ											

6. ジェットコースター　**jettokōsutā**　roller coaster

ジ	ェ	ッ	ト	コ	ー	ス	タ	ー						

7. キャッシュ　**kyasshu**　cash

キ	ャ	ッ	シ	ュ											

🎧 **F** Listen to the audio and fill each of the blanks with a katakana character. You can find the answers on page 125.

1.
		ル	

2.

3.

ラ
リ
ル
レ
ロ

Lesson 24

🎧 **A** Listen to the audio and practice saying the following five katakana characters.

Katakana	ラ	リ	ル	レ	ロ
Hiragana	ら	り	る	れ	ろ
Example words	ライオン lion	リスク risk	ルール rule	レストラン restaurant	ローション lotion

B Write the five katakana characters, paying attention to the order and the direction of each stroke.

ラ → ラ	ラ							
リ → リ	リ							
ノ → ル	ル							
レ	レ							
l → 冂 → ロ	ロ							

C Practice reading the following random sequences of characters. Pay attention to the elongation mark, voicing marks, p-marks, double consonants marked by the small ツ, and palatalized sounds (small ャ, ュ, or ョ)!

1. ラリラリル   ルレロラルレラ   ラレルロリ
2. ルロレーロ   レラリレラリレ   ロレラリル
3. シャラリスト   バロックデリデ   ポルミューズ

🎧 **D** Read the following words. Then use the audio to check your pronunciation. For a greater challenge, cover the English translation.

1. ライス   rice
2. リコール   recall
3. ルビー   ruby
4. チョコレート   chocolate
5. ロゴ   logo

E Listen to the audio and practice reading and writing the following words. For a greater challenge, cover the rōmaji and the English translation.

1. ラジオ **rajio** radio

ラ	ジ	オ									

2. リズム **rizumu** rhythm

リ	ズ	ム									

3. ルームメート **rūmumēto** roommate

ル	ー	ム	メ	ー	ト				

4. レシピ **reshipi** recipe

レ	シ	ピ									

5. ロビー **robī** lobby

ロ	ビ	ー									

6. タオル **taoru** towel

タ	オ	ル									

7. コロラド **Kororado** Colorado

コ	ロ	ラ	ド						

8. ラグビー **ragubī** rugby

ラ	グ	ビ	ー						

F Listen to the audio and fill each of the blanks with a katakana character. You can find the answers on page 125.

1. | | | | |
|---|---|---|---|

2. | | | ン |
|---|---|---|

3. | | | | |
|---|---|---|---|

ワ
ヲ
ン

Lesson 25

🎧 **A** Listen to the audio and practice saying the following katakana characters.

Katakana	ワ	ヲ	ン
Hiragana	わ	を	ん
Example words	ワルツ waltz		ダンス dance

B Write the five katakana characters, paying attention to the order and the direction of each stroke.

🎧 **C** Listen to the audio and practice reading and writing the following words. For a greater challenge, cover the rōmaji and the English translation.

1. ワクチン **wakuchin** vaccine

ワ	ク	チ	ン				

2. ワイシャツ **waishatsu** dress shirt

ワ	イ	シ	ャ	ツ			

3. ワイヤレス **waiyaresu** wireless

ワ	イ	ヤ	レ	ス			

4. ワシントン **washinton** Washington

ワ	シ	ン	ト	ン			

5. ワイドスクリーン **waidosukurīn** wide-screen

ワ	イ	ド	ス	ク	リ	ー	ン				

6. ハワイ　**hawai**　Hawaii

ハ	ワ	イ															

 **D** Listen to the audio and fill each of the blanks with a katakana character. You can find the answers on page 125.

1. | | | |
   |---|---|---|

2. | | | |
   |---|---|---|

3. | | | |
   |---|---|---|

E Practice reading the katakana characters as shown in this table as smoothly as possible. Start by reading the top line from left to right and work your way down the chart until you can memorize the order: ア イ ウ エ オ カ キ ク ケ コ, etc. This is the "alphabet" order used in Japanese dictionaries, so it's useful to know.

ア	イ	ウ	エ	オ	
カ	キ	ク	ケ	コ	
サ	シ	ス	セ	ソ	
タ	チ	ツ	テ	ト	
ナ	ニ	ヌ	ネ	ノ	
ハ	ヒ	フ	ヘ	ホ	
マ	ミ	ム	メ	モ	
ヤ		ユ		ヨ	
ラ	リ	ル	レ	ロ	
ワ				ヲ	ン

Lesson 26 Approximating foreign sounds

Words borrowed from Chinese are mostly written in kanji, especially those borrowed before the mid-20th century, but other foreign loan words are written in katakana. When there is a sequence of consonants in the foreign word that does not fit to the Japanese syllable structure, a vowel is inserted right after each problematic consonant. Usually, **o** is inserted after **t** or **d**; **i** is inserted after **ch** or **j**; and **u** is inserted after other consonants (e.g., street → **sutorīto**, punch → **panchi**).

🎧 **A** Listen to the audio and practice pronouncing and writing the following loan words.

1. beer ⇒ ビール
2. necktie ⇒ ネクタイ
3. scarf ⇒ スカーフ
4. street ⇒ ストリート
5. inch ⇒ インチ

To make the pronunciation of loan words closer to their original sound, the usage of katakana characters often violates the basic kana system you have just learned. For example, in addition to the small ヤ, ユ, and ヨ, used in the palatized sounds described on page 40, the small ア, イ, ウ, エ, and オ may be combined with a wider variety of characters (e.g., チェ, トゥ, ティ, ファ).

🎧 **B** Listen to the audio and practice pronouncing and writing the following words that include commonly used combinations of katakana characters.

1. シェリー **sherī** sherry

シェリー

2. ジェシカ **Jeshika** Jessica

ジェシカ

3. チェス **chesu** chess

チェス

4. モッツァレッラ **mottsarerra** mozzarella

モッツァレッラ

5. ティーシャツ **tīshatsu** T-shirt

ティ	ー	シャ	ツ								

6. ディナー **dinā** dinner

ディ	ナ	ー						

7. デュエット **duetto** duet

デュ	エ	ッ	ト					

8. ファン **fan** fan

ファ	ン							

9. フィアンセ **fianse** fiancé

フィ	ア	ン	セ				

10. フェリー **ferī** ferry

フェ	リ	ー					

11. フォーク **fōku** fork

フォ	ー	ク					

Note ウ with a voicing mark (ヴ) represents the "v" sound, and that the katakana for certain words can sometimes vary, as in the examples below.

1.	Yale	イェール	イエール	エール
2.	weight	ウェイト	ウエイト	
3.	whisky	ウィスキー	ウイスキー	
4.	vodka	ウォッカ	ウオッカ	
5.	violin	ヴァイオリン	バイオリン	
6.	Victoria	ヴィクトリア	ビクトリア	
7.	velvet	ヴェルヴェット	ベルベット	
8.	vocal	ヴォーカル	ボーカル	
9.	queen	クィーン	クイーン	
10.	question	クェスチョン	クエスチョン	
11.	quality	クォリティー	クオリティー	
12.	two	トゥー	ツー	

Lesson 27 Reading and writing basic words

A Listen to the audio and practice reading the words written in katakana. Once you have learned their meanings, cover the English and practice reading them again.

1. Vegetables & fruits

セロリ	celery
トマト	tomato
パイナップル	pineapple
バナナ	banana
ブルーベリー	blueberry
マッシュルーム	mushroom
レタス	lettuce

2. Sports

ゴルフ	golf
サッカー	soccer
スキー	skiing
スケート	skating
テニス	tennis
バスケットボール	basketball
バレーボール	volleyball

3. Musical instruments

ギター	guitar
チェロ	cello
ドラム	drums
バイオリン	violin
ピアノ	piano
フルート	flute
クラリネット	clarinet

4. Animals

ライオン	lion
キリン	giraffe
チーター	cheetah
パンダ	panda
ゴリラ	gorilla
チンパンジー	chimpanzee

5. Desserts

アイス	ice cream
ケーキ	cake
クッキー	cookies
チョコレート	chocolate

6. Foods

スパゲッティー	spaghetti
ピザ	pizza
ハンバーガー	hamburger
サンドイッチ	sandwich

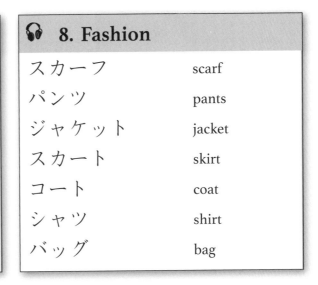

7. Drinks

コーヒー	coffee
ビール	beer
ウイスキー	whisky
ワイン	wine
オレンジジュース	orange juice
アイスティー	iced tea
カフェラテ	cafe latte

8. Fashion

スカーフ	scarf
パンツ	pants
ジャケット	jacket
スカート	skirt
コート	coat
シャツ	shirt
バッグ	bag

B Listen to the audio and write down the word you hear. The category that the word belongs to is specified in the brackets. Check your answers on page 125.

1. .... (vegetables)

2. .... (musical instruments)

3. .... (sports)

4. .... (desserts)

5. .... (drinks)

Lesson 28 People's names in katakana

🎧 **A** Listen to the audio and practice reading and writing the following common English family names in katakana.

1. カーター　**Kātā**　Carter

カ	ー	タ	ー													

2. スミス　**Sumisu**　Smith

ス	ミ	ス											

3. ジョンソン　**Jonson**　Johnson

ジ	ョ	ン	ソ	ン										

4. アンダーソン　**Andāson**　Anderson

ア	ン	ダ	ー	ソ	ン						

5. ミラー　**Mirā**　Miller

ミ	ラ	ー													

6. ブラウン　**Buraun**　Brown

ブ	ラ	ウ	ン												

🎧 **B** Listen to the audio and practice reading and writing the following common English male given names in katakana.

1. ジョージ　**Jōji**　George

ジ	ョ	ー	ジ												

2. ダニエル　**Danieru**　Daniel

ダ	ニ	エ	ル												

3. トーマス　**Tōmasu**　Thomas

ト	ー	マ	ス												

4. ベン　**Ben**　Ben

ベ	ン														

5. マイケル　**maikeru**　Michael

マ	イ	ケ	ル													

6. マシュー　**mashū**　Matthew

マ	シ	ュ	ー										

🎧 **C** Listen to the audio and practice reading and writing the following common English female given names in katakana.

1. アリソン　**Arison**　Alison

ア	リ	ソ	ン								

2. エリザベス　**Erizabesu**　Elizabeth

エ	リ	ザ	ベ	ス					

3. エマ　**Ema**　Emma

エ	マ												

4. ハナ　**Hana**　Hannah

ハ	ナ															

5. メーガン　**Mēgan**　Megan

メ	ー	ガ	ン								

6. リサ　**Risa**　Lisa

リ	サ															

🎧 **D** Listen to the audio and practice reading the names of famous people written in katakana. A fat dot called **nakaten** (中点) separates the family name and the given name. Do you recognize these famous names? You can find the answers on page 125.

1. マリリン・モンロー

2. ジョージ・ワシントン

3. ウイリアム・シェイクスピア

4. オプラ・ウィンフリー

5. オークワフィナ

6. イーロン・マスク

Lesson **29** Foreign place names

🎧 **A** Listen to the audio and practice reading and writing these country names in katakana. Then cover the rōmaji and the English and try reading again.

1. アメリカ **Amerika** USA

ア	メ	リ	カ										

2. イギリス **Igirisu** England

イ	ギ	リ	ス										

3. イタリア **Itaria** Italy

イ	タ	リ	ア										

4. インド **Indo** India

イ	ン	ド										

5. イラン **Iran** Iran

イ	ラ	ン										

6. オーストラリア **Ōsutoraria** Australia

オ	ー	ス	ト	ラ	リ	ア				

7. オランダ **Oranda** Holland

オ	ラ	ン	ダ										

8. カナダ **Kanada** Canada

カ	ナ	ダ										

9. ケニア **Kenia** Kenya

ケ	ニ	ア										

10. シンガポール **Shingapōru** Singapore

シ	ン	ガ	ポ	ー	ル							

11. スイス **Suisu** Switzerland

ス	イ	ス										

12. スペイン   **Supein**   Spain

スペイン

13. ロシア   **Roshia**   Russia

ロシア

14. ドイツ   **Doitsu**   Germany

ドイツ

15. ニュージーランド   **Nyūjīrando**   New Zealand

ニュージーランド

16. ブラジル   **Burajiru**   Brazil

ブラジル

17. フランス   **Furansu**   France

フランス

🎧 **B**   Listen to the audio and practice reading and writing these city names in katakana. Then cover the rōmaji and the English and try reading again.

1. イスタンブール   **Isutanbūru**   Istanbul

イスタンブール

2. カイロ   **Kairo**   Cairo

カイロ

3. サンフランシスコ   **Sanfuranshisuko**   San Francisco

サンフランシスコ

4. シカゴ   **Shikago**   Chicago

シカゴ

5. デリー   **Deri**   Delhi

デリー

6. トロント **Toronto** Toronto

| ト | ロ | ン | ト | | | | | | | | | | | | | | | |

7. ニューヨーク **Nyūyōku** New York

| ニ | ュ | ー | ヨ | ー | ク | | | | | | | | |

8. パリ **Pari** Paris

| パ | リ | | | | | | | | | | | | |

9. バンクーバー **Bankūbā** Vancouver

| バ | ン | ク | ー | バ | ー | | | | | | | | |

10. バンコク **Bankoku** Bangkok

| バ | ン | コ | ク | | | | | | | | | | |

11. ボストン **Bosuton** Boston

| ボ | ス | ト | ン | | | | | | | | | | |

12. ホンコン **Honkon** Hong Kong

| ホ | ン | コ | ン | | | | | | | | | | |

13. マドリッド **Madoriddo** Madrid

| マ | ド | リ | ッ | ド | | | | | | | | |

14. モントリオール **Montoriōru** Montreal

| モ | ン | ト | リ | オ | ー | ル | | | | |

15. ロサンゼルス **Rosanzerusu** Los Angeles

| ロ | サ | ン | ゼ | ル | ス | | | | | | | |

16. ローマ **Rōma** Rome

| ロ | ー | マ | | | | | | | | | |

17. ロンドン **Rondon** London

| ロ | ン | ド | ン | | | | | | | | | | |

Because katakana characters are not used for writing grammatical elements, you do not need to know rules and conventions to use them in sentences. As you have seen in the previous lessons, katakana is mainly used to represent words and names from foreign languages other than Chinese. Katakana is also used to represent sounds (onomatopoeia) as well as manners, physical states, and even psychological states (ideophones), although these words can sometimes be written in hiragana. Here are some examples:

キーキー	a sharp, squeaky noise
コロコロ	a small thing rolling
ゴロゴロ	a large thing rolling
カラカラ	extreme dryness
フワフワ	fluffiness and softness
ドキドキ	fast beating of one's heart

A Listen to the audio and practice reading the following sentences written in hiragana and katakana.

1. このベッドはキーキーいう。 (This bed is squeaking.)
2. ボールがコロコロころがった。 (A ball rolled.)
3. いわがゴロゴロころがった。 (A boulder rolled.)
4. のどがカラカラだ。 (My throat is parched; i.e., I'm very thirsty.)
5. フワフワのタオルをかった。 (I bought a fluffy towel.)
6. ドキドキしました。 (I got nervous.)

Katakana characters are also used for writing the names of plants and animals in business or academic contexts, although familiar plants and animals are commonly written in kanji or hiragana in daily life.

B Listen to the audio and practice reading the names of plants and animals common in Japan.

I. Plants

サクラ（さくら・桜）	cherry
ウメ（うめ・梅）	Japanese apricot
キク（きく・菊）	chrysanthemum
ツバキ（つばき・椿）	camellia
フジ（ふじ・藤）	wisteria

🎧 2. Animals

ウサギ （うさぎ・兎）	rabbit
ネコ （ねこ・猫）	cat
ネズミ （ねずみ・鼠）	mouse
タヌキ （たぬき・狸）	raccoon dog
キツネ （きつね・狐）	fox

Katakana is also used for aspects of pop culture (e.g., マンガ comic books) and company names (e.g., トヨタ Toyota, ヤマハ Yamaha) even if they have Japanese or Sino-Japanese origins.

🎧 **C** This self introduction was written in hiragana and katakana by Amy Chen. Read the passage aloud. Use the audio to copy correct intonation and rhythm.

> わたしはエミー・チェンです。しゅっしんはアメリカのニューヨークしゅうのロングアイランドです。いま、だいがくせいです。せんこうはコンピューター・サイエンスです。しゅみはコンピューターゲームと、アニメと、マンガです。

I'm Amy Chen. My birthplace is Long Island in the state of New York in the US. I'm a college student now. My major is computer science. My hobbies are [playing] computer games, [watching] anime, and [reading] comic books.

Vocabulary

わたし	I / me	いま	now
です	is / are	だいがくせい	university student
しゅっしん	birthplace	せんこう	major (subject)
しゅう	state	しゅみ	hobby
は	topic marker (pronounced "**wa**")	と	and

D Write your own self introduction, following the model above.

PART THREE

Kanji

How to learn kanji

Kanji is used to write words and names from Japanese and Chinese culture. This section introduces 50 kanji characters that are simple to write, frequently used in daily life and/or serve as both kanji characters and kanji radicals. Each kanji is provided with the following basic information:

1. Basic meaning.
2. Basic on-reading and kun-reading. The same kanji can be read in different ways. The on-reading is the approximation of the Chinese pronunciation of a character. The kun-reading is the pronunciation of the existing native Japanese word whose meaning is similar to the given character. The kun-reading may require some kana before or after the kanji to force the kanji to be read in a certain way. Such kana are provided in parentheses.
3. Radical. A kanji character is usually made up of multiple components, and one of them is designated as its radical. In a kanji dictionary, characters are sorted by radical.
4. Stroke count. Make sure you learn to write each kanji in the correct stroke order so you can write the character neatly and legibly.
5. Usage examples with hiragana reading, meaning and online audio (🎧) accessible through the link on page 12.
6. Mnemonics. Visual or verbal hints that will help you memorize the kanji.

Notes accompany many of the kanji characters to provide additional information on usage and related characters.

Before starting the lessons in this section, read the basic rules for writing kanji on page 83.

Use the online printable flash cards to help you memorize the characters (see link on page 12).

50 common kanji characters

Below are the 50 common kanji characters you will learn how to read and write in this section of the book. Their English meanings are given in this chart. You will learn the various ways of reading each kanji as you work your way through this section of the book.

一 one	二 two	三 three	四 four	五 five
山 mountain	川 river	木 tree, wood	林 woods	田 rice paddy
口 mouth	目 eye	足 foot / leg	手 hand	耳 ear
上 up, top, above	下 down, bottom, below, low	右 right	左 left	中 middle, center
百 a hundred	千 a thousand	万 ten thousand	円 Japanese yen, circle	金 gold, money
月 the moon, month	火 fire	水 water	土 soil, ground	日 the sun, day
見 look, view	行 go, perform, line	食 eat, food	飲 drink	書 write
赤 red	白 white	青 blue	黒 black	黄 yellow
大 big, great	小 small	高 high, tall, expensive	安 peaceful, cheap, safe	明 bright
男 (male) man	女 woman	人 person	子 child	犬 dog

How to write kanji

To write kanji properly and legibly, it's important to know how each stroke is drawn. There are basic principles and conventions for stroke endings, stroke direction, and stroke order.

STROKE ENDINGS

Each stroke ends in とめ (*tome*, stop), はね (*hane*, jump), or はらい (*harai*, sweep). (Note some diagonal lines end in stop-sweep.)

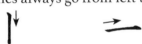

とめ **tome** (stop)   はね **hane** (jump)   はらい **harai** (sweep)

STROKE DIRECTION

A stroke can be vertical, horizontal, diagonal, angled or curved, or it can just be an abbreviated line.

Vertical lines always go from top to bottom, and horizontal lines always go from left to right.

Diagonal lines go downward or upward. For example:

If a stroke forms a corner, a sharp angle or a curve, it goes from left to right and then goes down, or goes down and then left to right. For example:

corner

sharp angle

curve

Some strokes have a combination of a sharp angle and a curve. For example:

Some strokes called てん (*ten*) are extremely short. They may be vertical or angled slightly:

STROKE ORDER

You must remember the order of the strokes in each character to write it neatly with the proper shape. Most kanji characters are written following the general principles of stroke order. These are as follows:

1. Kanji are written from top to bottom.

   三 (three)   一 二 三

2. Kanji are written from left to right.

   川 (river)   丿 川 川

3. Horizontal strokes usually precede vertical strokes when crossing, although there are some exceptions, such as 田.

   十 (ten)   一 十

4. A central line usually precedes the strokes placed on its right and left.

   小 (small)   亅 小 小

5. Three sides of a four-sided enclosure must be completed before finishing the inside. The bottom line of the enclosure must be completed at the very end.

   国 (country)   丨 冂 国 国

6. A right-to-left diagonal stroke precedes a left-to-right diagonal stroke.

   人 (person)   丿 人

7. A vertical line that runs through the center of a character is written last.

   車 (vehicle)   一 百 亘 車

8. A horizontal line that runs through the center of the character is written last.

   子 (child)   フ 了 子

一
二
三
四
五

Lesson **31** Numbers

In this lesson, you will learn the kanji characters for the first five numbers.

	一	二	三	四	五
Meaning	one	two	three	four	five
On-reading	いち, いつ	に	さん	し	ご
Kun-reading	ひと(つ)	ふた(つ)	み, みつ, みっ(つ)	よ, よ(つ), よっ(つ), よん	いつ, いつ(つ)
Radical	一	二	一	囗	二
Stroke count	1 stroke	2 strokes	3 strokes	5 strokes	4 strokes

🎧 Listen to the audio and practice reading and writing each of the five kanji.

→ 1

- 一　いち　one
- 一つ　ひとつ　one item
- 一月　いちがつ　January
- 一人　ひとり　one person
- 一時　いちじ　one o'clock
- 一分　いっぷん　one minute
- 統一　とういつ　uniformity

Mnemonic: 一 has only one stroke, and it means ONE.

Note: 一 also serves as the radical for 三 (three), 七 (seven), 世 (world) and other kanji.

→ 1　二 → 2

- 二　に　two
- 二つ　ふたつ　two items
- 二人　ふたり　two people
- 二月　にがつ　February
- 二時　にじ　2 o'clock

Mnemonic: 二 has two strokes, and it means TWO.

Note: 二 also serves as the radical for 五 (five), 云 (say) and other kanji.

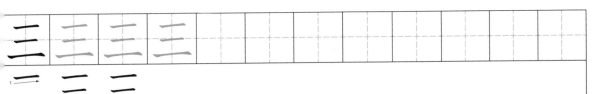

- 三 さん three
- 三つ みっつ three items
- 三月 さんがつ March
- 三人 さんにん three people
- 三時 さんじ three o'clock
- 三つ子 みつご triplets

Mnemonic: 三 has three strokes, and it means THREE.

四 四 四 四

- 四 よん four
- 四つ よっつ four items
- 四月 しがつ April
- 四時 よじ four o'clock
- 四人 よにん four people
- 四個 よんこ four pieces

Mnemonic: Remember a window with the curtains tied on either side.

Note: This kanji is pronounced し when quickly counting things or saying the numbers, but it is more often pronounced よん or よ, as し sounds like the word for "death" (死). 四月 (しがつ, April) is one of the exceptions.

- 五 ご five
- 五つ いつつ five items
- 五人 ごにん five people
- 五月 ごがつ May
- 五時 ごじ five o'clock
- 五日 いつか 5th (date)

Mnemonic: 五 has only four strokes, but it looks like it has FIVE lines in all.

山
川
木
林
田

Lesson 32 Parts of the landscape

In this lesson, you will learn five kanji characters that represent parts of the landscape.

	山	川	木	林	田
Meaning	mountain	river	tree, wood	woods	rice paddy
On-reading	さん	せん	もく, ぼく	りん	でん
Kun-reading	やま	かわ	き, こ	はやし	た
Radical	山	川	木	木	田
Stroke count	3 strokes	3 strokes	4 strokes	8 strokes	5 strokes

 Listen to the audio and practice reading and writing each of the five kanji.

- 山 やま mountain
- 富士山 ふじさん Mt. Fuji
- 火山 かざん volcano
- 山林 さんりん mountain forest
- 山田 やまだ Yamada (a common surname)

Mnemonic: 山 looks like a range of three MOUNTAINS.

- 川 かわ river
- 河川 かせん (multiple) rivers
- 川口 かわぐち Kawaguchi (a common surname)
- 小川 おがわ stream
- 川柳 せんりゅう senryu (humorous haiku)

Mnemonic: 川 looks like the flowing water of a RIVER.

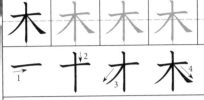

木 木 木 木

一 十 才 木

- 木 き tree
- 木曜日 もくようび Thursday
- 木陰 こかげ shade of a tree
- 大木 たいぼく large tree
- 木星 もくせい Jupiter

Mnemonic: The shape of 木 resembles a TREE.

Note: The radical 木 appears in 林 (woods), 森 (forest), 桜 (cherry), 梅 (plum), 桃 (peach), 杉 (cedar), 枝 (branches), 柳 (willow) and many other characters.

林 林 林 林

一 十 才 木 杧 村 材 林

- 林 はやし woods
- 山林 さんりん mountain forest
- 森林 しんりん forest; woods
- 植林 しょくりん afforestation

Mnemonic: Two 木 form the WOODS. These are not as dense as 森 (forest), which consists of three 木.

田 田 田 田

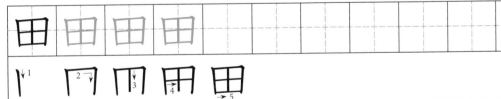
｜ 冂 冂 用 田

- 田 rice field
- 田畑 たはた fields (of rice and other crops)
- 水田 すいでん water-filled paddy field
- 油田 ゆでん oil field
- 田舎 いなか countryside

Mnemonic: 田 looks like a rice paddy.

Note: 田 also serves as the radical in the kanji for 男 (man), 町 (town), 畑 (cultivated field), 畜 (cattle) and other characters.

口目足手耳

Lesson 33 Parts of the body

In this lesson, you will learn five kanji characters for body parts.

	口	目	足	手	耳
Meaning	mouth	eye	foot / leg	hand	ear
On-reading	こう, く	もく, ぼく	そく	しゅ	じ
Kun-reading	くち	め, ま	あし, た(りる), た(す), た(る)	て	みみ
Radical	口	目	足	手	耳
Stroke count	3 strokes	5 strokes	7 strokes	4 strokes	6 strokes

🎧 Listen to the audio and practice reading and writing each of the five kanji.

- 口 くち mouth
- 出口 でぐち exit
- 入り口 いりぐち entrance
- 人口 じんこう population
- 口調 くちょう tone of voice

Mnemonic: The shape of 口 resembles a MOUTH that is open wide.

Note: 口 also serves as the radical in 叫 (shout), 吹 (blow), 呪 (curse), 呼 (call), 味 (taste), 喉 or 咽 (throat), and other mouth-related terms.

- 目 め eye
- 目的 もくてき purpose
- 目標 もくひょう goal
- 三つ目 みっつめ the third (piece)

Mnemonic: Can you see the character 目 in her eye?

Note: 目 also serves as the radical in 眼 (eye), 眉 (eyebrow), 眠 (sleep), 看 (care), 睡 (sleep), 瞬 (moment) and other kanji.

足

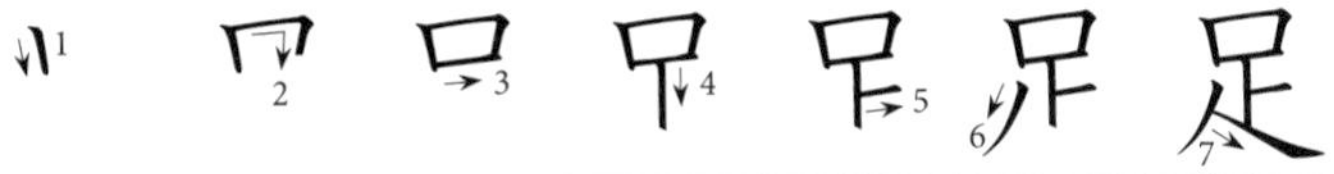

- 足　あし　leg
- 足りる　たりる　to be sufficient
- 足す　たす　to add
- 遠足　えんそく　an excursion

Mnemonic: Combine three characters: the kanji 口 (mouth), the katakana ト, and the kanji 人 (person) as you say "kuchi to hito" (口ト人).

Note: 足, slightly modified, serves as the radical in 跳 (jump), 路 (road), 跡 (trace) and other terms.

手

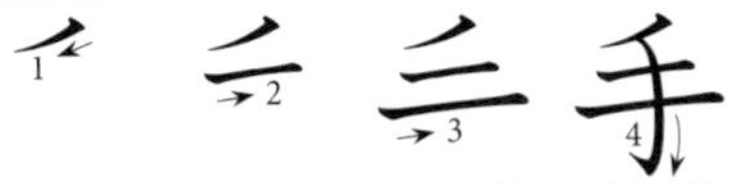

- 手　て　hand / arm
- 手紙　てがみ　letter
- 握手　あくしゅ　handshake
- 運転手　うんてんしゅ　driver
- 上手　じょうず　good (at)
- 下手　へた　poor (at)

Mnemonic: Can you see the character 手 in her hand?

Note: The radical 扌 (てへん), derived from 手, appears in 指 (finger), 持 (hold), 打 (hit), 払 (pay), 扱 (deal with), 投 (throw), and others.

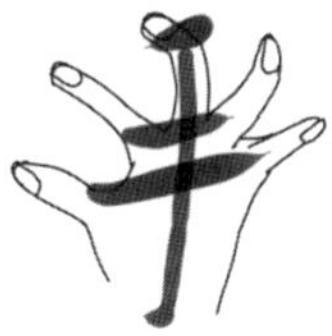

耳

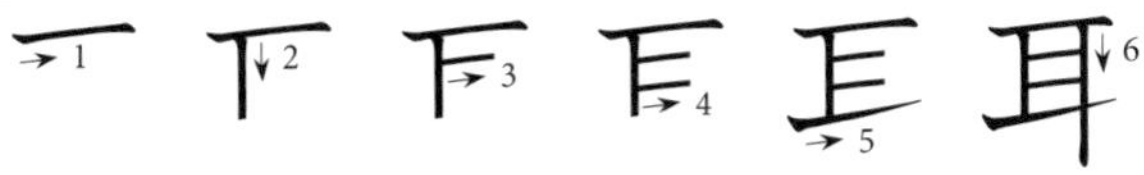

- 耳　みみ　ear
- 耳鼻咽喉科　じびいんこうか
  ear, nose and throat section

Mnemonic: Can you see the character 耳 in his ear?

Note: 耳 is also the radical in 聞 (listen), 聴 (listen), 職 (occupation), 聖 (saint) and other kanji.

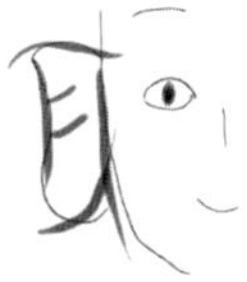

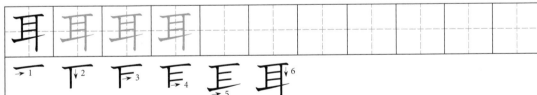

上
下
右
左
中

Lesson 34 Relative location

In this lesson, you will learn five kanji that represent relative locations.

	上	下	右	左	中
Meaning	up, top, above	down, bottom, below, low	right	left	middle, center
On-reading	じょう, しょう	か, げ	う, ゆう	さ	ちゅう, じゅう
Kun-reading	うえ, かみ、あ(がる), あ(げる), のぼ(る)	した, しも, もと, お(りる), おろ(す), くだ(さる), さ(がる), さ(げる)	みぎ	ひだり	なか
Radical	一	一	口	工	|
Stroke count	3 strokes	3 strokes	5 strokes	5 strokes	4 strokes

 Listen to the audio and practice reading and writing each of the five kanji.

上 上 上 上

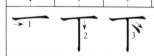

- 上 うえ top; up; above
- 上がる あがる to go up
- 上げる あげる to raise
- 上手 じょうず good (at)
- 上品 じょうひん refined
- 上り電車 のぼりでんしゃ inbound train

Mnemonic: Something is ABOVE the horizontal line.

下 下 下 下

- 下 した bottom/low/below
- 下さる くださる to give (honorific)
- 下り電車 くだりでんしゃ outbound train
- 地下 ちか basement

Mnemonic: Something is BELOW the horizontal line.

右 右 右 右

ノ ナ 右 右 右

- 右 みぎ right
- 右手 みぎて right hand
- 左右 さゆう left and right
- 右折 うせつ right turn
- 右翼 うよく right-wing (politics)

Mnemonic: You hold chopsticks (ナ) in your RIGHT hand and bring food to your mouth (口).

左 左 左 左

一 ナ 左 左 左

- 左 ひだり left
- 左手 ひだりて left hand
- 左右 さゆう left and right
- 左折 させつ left turn
- 左翼 さよく left-wing (politics)

Mnemonic: You hold your ruler in your LEFT hand and draw lines when you write the katakana エ.

中 中 中 中

- 中 なか inside
- 中心 ちゅうしん center
- 中学校 ちゅうがっこう middle school
- 年中 ねんじゅう year round
- 世界中 せかいじゅう all over the world
- 中国 ちゅうごく China

Mnemonic: There is a bar (|) in the MIDDLE.

百
千
万
円
金

Lesson **35** Large numbers and money

In this lesson, you will learn the kanji for three large numbers that are often used in Japanese text to express prices, amounts and quantities. In addition, you will learn the currency unit used in Japan, as well as the kanji that means gold, money and metal.

	百	千	万	円	金
Meaning	a hundred	a thousand	ten thousand	Japanese yen, circle	gold, money
On-reading	ひゃく	せん	まん, ばん	えん	きん, こん
Kun-reading		ち		まる(い)	かね, かな
Radical	白	十	一	冂	金
Stroke count	6 strokes	3 strokes	3 strokes	4 strokes	8 strokes

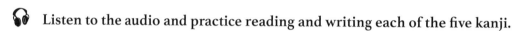 Listen to the audio and practice reading and writing each of the five kanji.

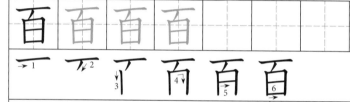

- 百 ひゃく one hundred
- 百円 ひゃくえん 100 yen
- 三百円 さんびゃくえん 300 yen
- 六百円 ろっぴゃくえん 600 yen

Mnemonic: Combine the two kanji characters 一 (one) and 白 (white). Someone gave me one (一) hundred-dollar bill in a white (白) envelope.

Note: 百 is pronounced ひゃく, びゃく, or ぴゃく, depending on the number that precedes it.

- 千 せん one thousand
- 三千人 さんぜんにん 3,000 people
- 八千人 はっせんにん 8,000 people
- 千鳥 ちどり plover
- 千羽鶴 せんばづる 1,000 paper cranes

Mnemonic: Topping 十 (ten) with a curvy stroke increases its value and turns it into a THOUSAND.

Note: 千 is pronounced as せん or ぜん depending on the number that precedes it.

万 万 万 万

- 一万 いちまん ten thousand
- 三万 さんまん 30,000
- 万年筆 まんねんひつ fountain pen
- 万能 ばんのう all-purpose
- 万歳 ばんざい banzai
- 千差万別 せんさばんべつ
  wide-ranging variation (idiom)

Mnemonic: 万 has only three strokes, but it means TEN THOUSAND.

円 円 円 円

|¹ ⌐² ⌐³ 円⁴

- 円 えん circle; yen
- 五百円 ごひゃくえん 500 yen
- 円い まるい round
- 円周 えんしゅう circumference
- 楕円 だえん oval
- 半円 はんえん semicircle

Mnemonic: Let's put two 500 YEN big ROUND Japanese coins in the two square slots in this coin-collector's panel.

Note: The pronunciation of 円 in Japanese is えん ("en"), not いえん ("yen").

金 金 金 金

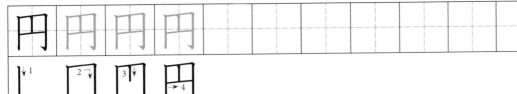

- 金 きん gold
- 金曜日 きんようび Friday
- お金 おかね money
- 金具 かなぐ metal fittings
- 針金 はりがね wire
- 金色 こんじき gold color

Mnemonic: A miner went to the mountain and got two big nuggets of GOLD!

Note: 金 also serves as the radical in 針 (needle), 銀 (silver), 銅 (copper), 鉄 (iron), 鉛 (lead), 鋼 (steel) and other characters.

月
火
水
土
日

Lesson 36 Days of the week

You learned 木 and 金 (used in the words Thursday and Friday) in lessons 32 and 35. Now you will learn five additional kanji characters so that you can write the seven days of the week in kanji.

	月	火	水	土	日
Meaning	the moon, month	fire	water	soil, ground	the sun, day
On-reading	がつ, げつ	か	スイ	と, ど	にち, じつ
Kun-reading	つき	ひ	みず	つち	か, ひ
Radical	月	火	水	土	日
Stroke count	4 strokes	4 strokes	4 strokes	3 strokes	4 strokes

🎧 Listen to the audio and practice reading and writing each of the five kanji.

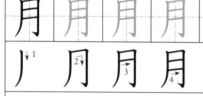

- 月 つき moon
- 月曜日 げつようび Monday
- 三月 さんがつ March
- 今月 こんげつ this month
- 来月 らいげつ next month
- 先月 せんげつ last month
- 満月 まんげつ full moon
- 月給 げっきゅう salary

Mnemonic: 月 looks like the crescent MOON.

Note: 月 also serves as the radical in the kanji 朝 (morning), 有 (exist) and 期 (term), among others.

- 火 ひ fire
- 火曜日 かようび Tuesday
- 火山 かざん volcano
- 火事 かじ fire, conflagration
- 花火 はなび fireworks

Mnemonic: It's a camp FIRE.

Note: 火 also serves as the radical in 炊 (cook), 焼 (grill), 煙 (smoke), 燃 (burn), 灯 (torch), and 炉 (furnace).

水 水 水 水

ヺ¹ ヺ² 水³ 水⁴

- 水 みず water
- 水曜日 すいようび Wednesday
- 水星 すいせい Mercury
- 水道水 すいどうすい tap water
- 洪水 こうずい flooding

Mnemonic: 水 looks like the WATER coming out of a tap with splashes.

Note: 水 also serves as the radical in other kanji, including 氷 (ice), 永 (eternity) and 泳 (swim).

土 土 土 土

一¹ 十² 土³

- 土 つち soil
- 土曜日 どようび Saturday
- 粘土 ねんど clay
- 土地 とち land
- 土星 どせい Saturn

Mnemonic: The shape of 土 resembles two layers of soil; you check the depth by sticking a long bar into them.

Note: 土 also serves as the radical in 地 (ground), 坂 (hill), 場 (place) and other kanji.

日 日 日 日

ﾄ¹ 冂² 日³ 日⁴

- 日 ひ sun; day
- 日曜日 にちようび Sunday
- 日光 にっこう sunshine
- 日本 にほん or にっぽん Japan
- 二日 ふつか two days; 2nd (date)
- 平日 へいじつ weekday
- 休日 きゅうじつ holiday; day off

Mnemonic: 日 looks like a square sun with a long sunspot.

Note: 日 also serves as the radical in 早 (early), 明 (bright), 暗 (dark), 春 (spring), 時 (time), 晴 (clear sky), 星 (star), 昇 (rise), 暑 (hot) and other kanji.

Lesson **37** Actions

In this lesson, you will learn the kanji for five verbs that represent basic actions. Make sure you memorize the hiragana verb endings (*okurigana*) correctly.

	見	行	食	飲	書
Meaning	look, view	go, perform; line	eat; food	drink	write
On-reading	けん	ぎょう, こう, あん	しょく, じき	いん	しょ
Kun-reading	み(る), み(える), み(せる)	い(く), おこな(う), ゆ(く)	た(べる), く(う)	の(む)	か(く)
Radical	見	行	食	食	日
Stroke count	7 strokes	6 strokes	9 strokes	12 strokes	10 strokes

🎧 Listen to the audio and practice reading and writing each of the five kanji.

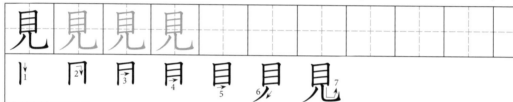

- 見る みる to look
- 見える みえる to see
- 見せる みせる to show
- 発見 はっけん discovery
- 意見 いけん opinion

Mnemonic: To have a close LOOK at something on the floor, you bend your legs (儿) so your eyes (目) are near it.

Note: 見 also serves as the radical in 覚 (memorize), 親 (parent), 観 (observe) and other kanji.

- 行く いく to go
- 行 ぎょう line (of text)
- 行う おこなう to perform
- 旅行 りょこう trip
- 銀行 ぎんこう bank
- 行事 ぎょうじ event

Mnemonic: 行 appears to have two paths that one can GO and walk on.

Note: 行 also serves as the radical in 街 (boulevard), 衛 (protection), 衝 (thrust) and other kanji.

食 食 食 食

イ ㇒ ㇏ 今 今 食 食 食 食

- 食べる たべる to eat
- 食う くう to eat (informal word)
- 食事 しょくじ food; meal
- 定食 ていしょく set menu
- 洋食 ようしょく Western-style food
- 断食 だんじき fasting

Mnemonic: Combine the component that looks like a roof (ㇸ) and the kanji "good" (良). It is always "good" to EAT under a roof or tent so you don't get bugs in your FOOD.

Note: 食 also serves as the radical in 飲 (drink), 飯 (cooked rice), 餅 (mochi), 餌 (bait), 飼 (domesticate), 飢 (starvation), 養 (nurture) and other kanji.

飲 飲 飲 飲

イ ㇒ ㇏ 今 今 食 食 食 飲 飲 飲 飲

- 飲む のむ to drink
- 飲み物 のみもの drink (noun)
- 飲料 いんりょう beverage
- 飲酒運転 いんしゅうんてん drunk driving

Mnemonic: Combine the "eat" radical (食) and the kanji for "to lack" (欠). You can't "eat" this food, as it "lacks" solids—you'll have to DRINK it.

書 書 書 書

㇆ ㇕ ㇕ 肀 肀 聿 聿 書 書 書

- 書く かく to write
- 書道 しょどう calligraphy
- 読書 どくしょ reading
- 書店 しょてん bookstore
- 図書館 としょかん library

Mnemonic: I WROTE STORIES (日) on small sheets for a week. I'll lay them flat and stick an ice pick through them so I won't lose them.

Lesson 38 Colors

In this lesson, you will learn five kanji characters that represent colors.

	赤	白	青	黒	黄
Meaning	red	white	blue	black	yellow
On-reading	せき, しゃく	はく, びゃく	せい, しょう	こく	おう, こう
Kun-reading	あか, あか(い)	しろ, しら, しろ(い)	あお, あお(い)	くろ, くろ(い)	き, こ
Radical	赤	白	青	黒	黄
Stroke count	7 strokes	5 strokes	8 strokes	11 strokes	11 strokes

🎧 **Listen to the audio and practice reading and writing each of the five kanji.**

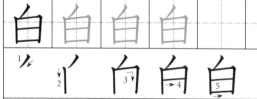

- 赤 あか red (noun)
- 赤い あかい red (adj.)
- 赤ちゃん あかちゃん baby
- 赤字 あかじ in the red
- 赤道 せきどう equator
- 赤血球 せっけっきゅう red blood cell

Mnemonic: Write 土 (soil) and add four short strokes in different shapes hanging under it.

Note: 赤 also serves as the radical in 赦 (forgive) and other kanji.

- 白 しろ white (noun)
- 白い しろい white (adj.)
- 白髪 しらが or はくはつ gray hair
- 白夜 びゃくや white night
- 卵白 らんぱく egg white

Mnemonic: Combine the katakana ノ and the kanji 日 (sun).

Note: 白 also serves as the radical in 百 (one hundred), 的 (target), 皆 (all), 皇 (emperor) and other kanji.

青 青 青 青

ー₁ 二₂ 三₃ 丰₄ 寺₅ 青₆ 青₇ 青₈

- 青　あお　blue (noun)
- 青い　あおい　blue (adj.)
- 青春　せいしゅん　adolescent
- 青年　せいねん　youth; young man

Mnemonic: I covered the moon (月) with three plastic sheets and nailed them in the middle to turn the moonlight BLUE!

Note: 青 also serves as the radical in 静 (stillness) and other kanji.

黒 黒 黒 黒

丨₁ 冂₂ 囗₃ 曱₄ 甲₅ 罒₆ 里₇ 里₈ 黒₉ 黒₁₀ 黒₁₁

- 黒　くろ　black (noun)
- 黒い　くろい　black (adj.)
- 黒板　こくばん　blackboard
- 黒字　くろじ　in the black

Mnemonic: Write 田, put 土 under it and add four dots.

Note: 黒 also serves as the radical in 黙 (silence) and other kanji.

黄 黄 黄 黄

一₁ 十₂ 廿₃ 井₄ 共₅ 昔₆ 苗₇ 苗₈ 黄₉ 黄₁₀ 黄₁₁

- 黄色　きいろ　yellow (noun)
- 黄色い　きいろい　yellow (adj.)
- 卵黄　らんおう　egg yolk
- 黄金色　こがねいろ　golden

Mnemonic: This kanji is almost horizontally symmetrical.

Lesson **39** Adjectives

In this lesson, you will learn five kanji characters that are used to describe things.

	大	小	高	安	明
Meaning	big, great	small	high, tall, expensive	peaceful, cheap, safe	bright
On-reading	だい, たい	しょう	こう	あん	みょう, めい
Kun-reading	おお, おお(きい)	ちい(さい), お, こ	たか(い), たか, たか(める), たか(まる)	やす(い)	あか(るい), あき(らか), あ(ける)
Radical	大	小	高	宀	日
Stroke count	3 strokes	3 strokes	10 strokes	6 strokes	8 strokes

 Listen to the audio and practice reading and writing each of the five kanji.

大 大 大 大

一 ナ 大

- 大きい おおきい big
- 大学 だいがく university
- 大文字 おおもじ capital letters
- 大切 たいせつ important

Mnemonic: The shape of 大 resembles a person stretching out the arms to indicate BIG.

Note: 大 also serves as the radical in 太 (thick), 奥 (interior) and other kanji.

小 小 小 小

亅 小 小

- 小さい ちいさい small
- 小学校 しょうがっこう elementary school
- 小川 おがわ stream; brook
- 小鳥 ことり small bird

Mnemonic: The shape of 小 resembles someone who is trying to look SMALL by crouching.

Note: 小 also serves as the radical in 少 (few, a little) and other kanji.

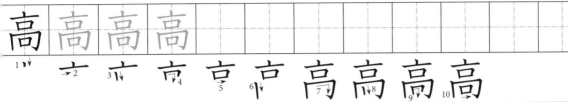

- 高い　たかい　tall; high
- 背が高い　せがたかい　tall (people and animals)
- 高まる　たかまる　to rise
- 高める　たかめる　to raise
- 高校　こうこう　high school
- 高速道路　こうそくどうろ　highway

Mnemonic: 高 looks like an ancient TALL tower.

- 安い　やすい　cheap
- 安全　あんぜん　safety
- 安心　あんしん　peace of mind
- 治安　ちあん　public safety
- 安らか　やすらか　peaceful

Mnemonic: If the house has a roof (宀) and a woman (女), it is PEACEFUL.

- 明るい　あかるい　bright
- 透明　とうめい　transparent
- 照明　しょうめい　lighting
- 文明　ぶんめい　civilization
- 明日　あす or みょうにち　tomorrow

Mnemonic: When the sun (日) and the moon (月) are placed side by side, it will be very BRIGHT.

Lesson 40 Living beings

In this lesson, you will learn five kanji characters that symbolize living beings.

	男	女	人	子	犬
Meaning	(male) man	woman	person	child	dog
On-reading	だん, なん	じょ, にょ, にゅう	じん, にん	し, す	けん
Kun-reading	おとこ	おんな, め	ひと	こ	いぬ
Radical	田	女	人	子	犬
Stroke count	7 strokes	3 strokes	2 strokes	3 strokes	4 strokes

🎧 Listen to the audio and practice reading and writing each of the five kanji.

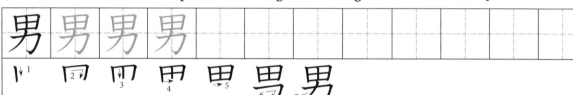

- 男 おとこ man
- 長男 ちょうなん eldest son
- 次男 じなん second son
- 男性 だんせい man (formal)

Mnemonic: The strength (力) in a rice paddy (田) symbolized MAN in the old days.

- 女 おんな woman
- 長女 ちょうじょ eldest daughter
- 次女 じじょ second daughter
- 女神 めがみ goddess
- 女房 にょうぼう (one's own) wife

Mnemonic: Combine the three letters, the hiragana く, the katakana ノ, and the kanji 一 (one), as you say "ku-no-ichi." (くノ一).

Note: 女 serves as the radical in 姉 (older sister), 妹 (younger sister), 娘 (daughter), 姫 (princess), 好 (favorite), 妻 (wife) and other kanji.

人 人 人 人

ノ 人

- 人 ひと person
- 人間 にんげん human being
- 日本人 にほんじん Japanese person
- 人種 じんしゅ race, ethnicity
- 個人 こじん individual
- 人形 にんぎょう doll
- 病人 びょうにん sick person

Mnemonic: 人 resembles a standing PERSON without the head and arms.

Note: イ (にんべん) derived from 人 serves as the radical in 休 (rest), 体 (body), 侍 (samurai) and other kanji.

子 子 子 子

了 了 子

- 子供 こども child
- 妻子 さいし wife and children
- お菓子 おかし sweets, snacks
- 子孫 しそん offspring
- 椅子 いす chair
- 扇子 せんす folding fan

Mnemonic: The shape of the kanji 子 resembles a CHILD swaddled in cloth as a baby.

Note: 子 also serves as the radical in 字 (script / character), 学 (learning), 孫 (grandchild), 孝 (filial piety) and other kanji.

犬 犬 犬 犬

一 ナ 大 犬

- 犬 いぬ dog
- 子犬 こいぬ puppy
- 番犬 ばんけん watchdog
- 犬歯 けんし eye tooth

Mnemonic: A big (大) DOG with a "spot" on the upper right-hand corner of his face.

Note: 犬 also serves as the radical in 獣 (beast), 献 (offering), 獄 (prison) and other kanji.

Lesson 41 Radicals

A kanji character is made up of one or more components, one of which is designated as the "radical." Radicals are used to categorize or index kanji characters, for example, in dictionaries. There are 214 kanji radicals in Japanese, based on those traditionally used in the Chinese language. Radicals are commonly known as bushu (部首) in Japanese. They are grouped into the following seven categories, depending on the position they occupy within a character:

	Category	Position	Example radical and kanji that include it
1.	へん	left	日 (ひへん or にちへん) 明 bright, 暗 dark, 時 time, 晩 evening
2.	かんむり	top	艹 (くさかんむり) 花 flower, 草 grass, 葉 leaves, 薬 medicine 若 young, 苦 bitter, 茶 tea
3.	あし	bottom	儿 (ひとあし) 光 light, 先 ahead, 兄 older brother
4.	つくり	right	力 (ちから) 動 move, 助 help, 功 achievement
5.	かまえ	outside	囗 (くにがまえ) 国 country, 困 trouble, 回 rotate, 四 four
6.	たれ	left and top	疒 (やまいだれ) 病 sickness, 痛 painful, 症 symptoms, 癌 cancer
7.	にょう	left and bottom	辶 (しんにょう) 道 road, 通 pass, 速 fast, 近 near, 遠 far

A In the following pairs of kanji, name the radical that is being shared. You can find the answers on page 126.

1. 明るい   bright   暗い   dark   ....

2. 通る   to pass through   道   street   ....

3. 薬   medicine   苦い   bitter   ....

4.	助ける	to help	動く	to move	....
5.	先生	teacher	お兄さん	elder brother	....
6.	国	country	困る	to be in trouble	....
7.	病	illness	癌	cancer	....

B One of the most frequently used radicals is さんずいへん（氵）, which is found in nearly 100 kanji characters. Most have meanings that are related to water. Look at the following kanji words and circle the ones that have さんずいへん. You can find the answers on page 126.

山	mountain	涙	tears	病気	illness	海	ocean
川	river	河	river	湖	lake	明るい	bright
林	woods	お酒	liquor	港	harbor	漁	fishing
田	rice paddy	金	gold	黒	black	青	blue
漢字	kanji	泳ぐ	to swim	洗う	wash	洪水	flooding

Lesson 42 People's names in kanji

Japanese family names usually consist of one, two, or three kanji characters. The following are examples of kanji used for common family names in Japan (with hiragana readings in brackets):

森 （もり）	林 （はやし）	谷 （たに）
鈴木 （すずき）	佐藤 （さとう）	田中 （たなか）
山本 （やまもと）	渡辺 （わたなべ）	高橋 （たかはし）
小林 （こばやし）	伊藤 （いとう）	松田 （まつだ）
小河原 （おがわら）	長谷川 （はせがわ）	久保田 （くぼた）

Most given names for males in Japan consist of one, two, or three kanji characters. For example:

正 （ただし）	真 （まこと）	賢治 （けんじ）
良夫 （よしお）	健一 （けんいち）	健次郎 （けんじろう）
昌太郎 （しょうたろう）	望 （のぞむ）	

Most given names for females in Japan consist of one, two, or three kanji characters. Many of them end in 子 （こ）, especially since the Second World War. For example:

幸 （さち）	雪 （ゆき）	香 （かおり）
紗耶香 （さやか）	友恵 （ともえ）	由里 （ゆり）
由美子 （ゆみこ）	純子 （じゅんこ）	智恵子 （ちえこ）
陽子 （ようこ）	洋子 （ようこ）	良子 （よしこ）
真理子 （まりこ）	恵美子 （えみこ）	可奈子 （かなこ）

Some given names are written only in hiragana or partially in hiragana. Some names are written in katakana, although this is not very common.

Practice reading these family names written with kanji you have learned. The reading of personal names varies. For example, 高田 can be たかだ or たかた.

林 （はやし）	田中 （たなか）	山田 （やまだ）
川口 （かわぐち）	山中 （やまなか）	中山 （なかやま）
黒川 （くろかわ）	黒田 （くろだ）	大山 （おおやま）
安田 （やすだ）	高田 （たかだ）	小山 （こやま）
金田 （かねだ）	山川 （やまかわ）	小林 （こばやし）
青木 （あおき）	青山 （あおやま）	白川 （しらかわ）
大川 （おおかわ）	中川 （なかがわ）	小川 （おがわ）
高木 （たかぎ）	山口 （やまぐち）	中田 （なかだ）

🎧 **A** Practice writing the following Japanese family names in **kanji**.

1. 小林　こばやし

小	林										

2. 山田　やまだ

山	田										

3. 大山　おおやま

大	山										

4. 黒川　くろかわ

黒	川										

5. 青木　あおき

青	木										

6. 安田　やすだ

安	田										

7. 高木　たかぎ

高	木										

B Use your best guess and match the family names written in kanji in Box A with their pronunciations written in hiragana in Box B. You can find the answers on page 126.

1. 金田	a. あおき
2. 中山	b. なかやま
3. 青木	c. くろかわ
4. 黒川	d. かねだ
5. 林	e. はやし

Lesson 43 Place names in kanji

🎧 **A** Listen to the audio and practice reading the names of the following countries shown on the map.

1. 中国 （ちゅうごく） China
2. 北朝鮮 （きたちょうせん） North Korea
3. 韓国 （かんこく） South Korea
4. 上海 （しゃんはい） Shanghai
5. 日本 （にほん or にっぽん） Japan
6. 台湾 （たいわん） Taiwan
7. 香港 （ほんこん） Hong Kong

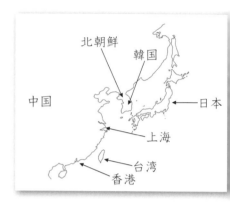

🎧 **B** Listen to the audio and practice reading the names of the four main islands of Japan.

1. 本州 （ほんしゅう）
2. 北海道 （ほっかいどう）
3. 九州 （きゅうしゅう）
4. 四国 （しこく）

🎧 **C** Listen to the audio and practice reading the names of some of the largest cities in Japan.

1. 東京 （とうきょう）
2. 横浜 （よこはま）
3. 大阪 （おおさか）
4. 名古屋 （なごや）
5. 札幌 （さっぽろ）
6. 神戸 （こうべ）
7. 京都 （きょうと）
8. 福岡 （ふくおか）

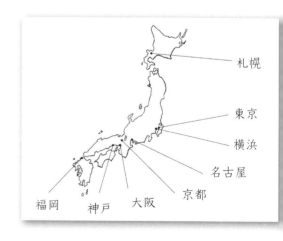

🎧 **D** The Yamanote-sen (山手線) is one of the busiest railway lines in Tokyo, connecting many of the major areas. Practice reading the names of the 30 stations of the Yamanote line as you go around the map clockwise, starting with Tokyo, top center.

1. 東京（とうきょう）
2. 有楽町（ゆうらくちょう）
3. 新橋（しんばし）
4. 浜松町（はままつちょう）
5. 田町（たまち）
6. 高輪ゲートウェイ（たかなわげーとうぇい）
7. 品川（しながわ）
8. 大崎（おおさき）
9. 五反田（ごたんだ）
10. 目黒（めぐろ）
11. 恵比寿（えびす）
12. 渋谷（しぶや）
13. 原宿（はらじゅく）
14. 代々木（よよぎ）
15. 新宿（しんじゅく）

16. 新大久保（しんおおくぼ）
17. 高田馬場（たかだのばば）
18. 目白（めじろ）
19. 池袋（いけぶくろ）
20. 大塚（おおつか）
21. 巣鴨（すがも）
22. 駒込（こまごめ）
23. 田端（たばた）
24. 西日暮里（にしにっぽり）
25. 日暮里（にっぽり）
26. 鶯谷（うぐいすだに）
27. 上野（うえの）
28. 御徒町（おかちまち）
29. 秋葉原（あきはばら）
30. 神田（かんだ）

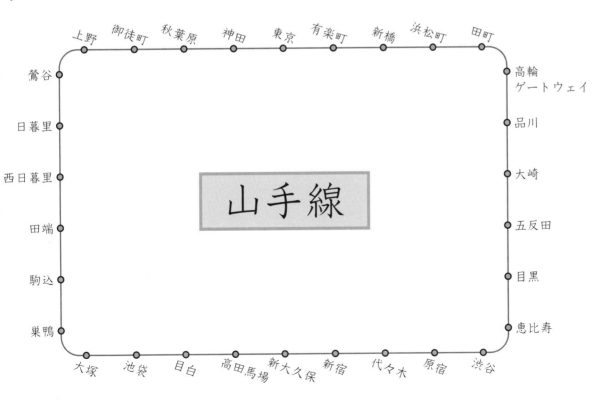

Lesson 44 Reading basic words

🎧 **Listen to the audio and practice reading the kanji words in each thematic group.**

🎧 1. Schools

小学校（しょうがっこう）	elementary school
中学校（ちゅうがっこう）	middle school
高校（こうこう）	high school
大学（だいがく）	university
大学院（だいがくいん）	graduate school

🎧 2. Stores

本屋（ほんや）	bookstore
肉屋（にくや）	butcher shop
魚屋（さかなや）	fishmonger
花屋（はなや）	flower shop
酒屋（さかや）	liquor store

🎧 3. Temperature

暑い（あつい）	hot (weather, temperature)
熱い（あつい）	hot (liquid or solid)
寒い（さむい）	cold (weather, temperature)
冷たい（つめたい）	cold (liquid or solid)
暖かい（あたたかい）	warm (weather, temperature)
温かい（あたたかい）	warm (liquid or solid)
涼しい（すずしい）	cool (weather, temperature)

🎧 4. School subjects

文学（ぶんがく）	literature
数学（すうがく）	mathematics
社会学（しゃかいがく）	sociology
経済学（けいざいがく）	economics

🎧 6. Compass directions

東（ひがし）	east
西（にし）	west
北（きた）	north
南（みなみ）	south

🎧 5. Hobbies

茶道（さどう）	tea ceremony
書道（しょどう）	calligraphy
華道（かどう）	flower arranging

🎧 7. Family

The first pronunciation is used to refer to someone else's family member. The second is used when referring to one's own family member in front of others.

お父さん・父（おとうさん・ちち）	father
お母さん・母（おかあさん・はは）	mother
お兄さん・兄（おにいさん・あに）	older brother
お姉さん・姉（おねえさん・あね）	older sister
弟さん・弟（おとうとさん・おとうと）	younger brother
妹さん・妹（いもうとさん・いもうと）	younger sister

Writing sentences and paragraphs Lesson 45

🎧 **A** Listen to the audio and practice reading the phrases and sentences. Next, practice writing them yourself. Find the rōmaji and English translations on page 126.

1. 山と川

2. 左と右

3. 上と下

4. 目と口

5. 手と足

6. これは高いです。

7. あの山を見てください。とても高い山です。

8. これは三万円です。あれは五千円です。

9. あの男の人は青木さんです。あの女の人は小林さんです。

10. みそしるを飲みました。それから、すしを食べました。

11. わたしのかばんは赤いです。でも、大山さんのは黒いです。

🎧 **B** Listen to the audio and practice reading the following journal entry written by Yukiko. Next, practice writing it out yourself.

きょうは、デパートに行った。青のセーターをかった。ちょっと高かった。二万円だった。でも、とてもきれいで、きにいってしまった。明子に見せたら、「めちゃかわいい。」といった。またアルバイトをしてお金をためよう。

I went to the department store today. I bought a blue sweater. It was a bit expensive. It was 20,000 yen. But it was really pretty, and I fell in love with it. When I showed it to Akiko, she said, "It's super cute!" I'll save up money again by working part-time.

Vocabulary

きょう	today	とても	really
は	topic marker (pronounced "**wa**")	きれい	pretty
		きにいってしまった	fell in love with (a thing)
デパート	department store	めちゃ	super (slang)
に	to	かわいい	cute
行った	went	いった	said
かった	bought	また	again
ちょっと	a bit	アルバイト	part-time job
だった	was	ためよう	will save
でも	but		

REVIEW

Congratulations! You've mastered all the hiragana and katakana characters along with 50 basic kanji characters! Through this process, you've also learned the authentic pronunciation of all possible Japanese sounds and hundreds of basic Japanese vocabulary words, using your eyes, ears, mouth, and hands!

You still need to learn more kanji, but you are well equipped to do this now that you know 50 basic kanji characters, many radicals, and the basic principles of the structure of kanji. Check out some Internet kanji dictionaries and simple search engines to find additional meanings and usage of kanji. Be creative and continue to enjoy learning!

Review the 45 lessons one more time and then challenge yourself to the review exercises on the following pages.

Review Exercises

🎧 **1** Read the following words for Japanese foods written in hiragana. If you don't know what some of the words mean, look them up online.

1. すし

2. しゃぶしゃぶ

3. すきやき

4. うなぎ

5. さしみ

6. みそしる

7. てんぷら

8. たこやき

9. おこのみやき

10. おにぎり

2 Hidden in the wordsearch below are the names of six Japanese foods. Can you find them? The six words are all in the previous exercise. You can find the answers on page 126.

う	な	ぎ	く	す
ま	す	は	に	き
さ	し	み	な	や
み	そ	し	る	き
う	て	ん	ぷ	ら

🎧 **3** The following are two well-known tongue twisters in Japanese. Read them as fast as you can.

a. すもも　　も　　　　もも　　も　　　　　　もも　　　の　　うち
　 plum　　also　　　peach　　also　　　　peach　　's　　family

"Both plums and peaches belong to the peach family."

b. なま　　むぎ　　　なま　　ごめ　　　　なま　　たまご
　 raw　　wheat　　raw　　rice　　　　raw　　egg

"Raw wheat, raw rice and raw eggs!"

🎧 **4** Read the katakana words in the box on the left and match them with the English words in the box on the right. You can find the answers on page 126.

1. セーター	a. bus
2. バス	b. test
3. テスト	c. sweater
4. ソーセージ	d. ice cream
5. アイス	e. sausage

5 Can you read the names of these countries? Find the answers on page 127.

1. エジプト
2. イタリア
3. カナダ
4. タイ
5. アメリカ
6. スペイン
7. ドイツ
8. イギリス
9. インド
10. チリ
11. オーストラリア
12. フランス
13. ブラジル
14. ロシア

6 Can you find the names of eight countries in this wordsearch? The eight words are all in the previous exercise. You can find the answers on page 127.

ロ	サ	ス	フ	イ
シ	イ	ペ	ク	タ
ア	タ	イ	チ	リ
フ	ラ	ン	ス	ア
プ	マ	ド	イ	ツ

7 Below is the menu of a fast-food restaurant. Study it carefully and answer the questions on page 117. You can find the answers on page 127.

ハンバーガー メニュー		
	ハンバーガー	¥250
	ビッグバーガー	¥280
	チーズバーガー	¥280
	ダブルチーズバーガー	¥290
	テリヤキバーガー	¥280
	テリヤキチキンバーガー	¥290
	フィッシュバーガー	¥290

ドリンク メニュー	コールドドリンク			
	コーラ	(S) ¥100	(M) ¥180	(L) ¥200
	ジンジャエール	(S) ¥100	(M) ¥180	(L) ¥200
	メロンソーダ	(S) ¥100	(M) ¥180	(L) ¥200
	オレンジジュース	¥100		
	アップルジュース	¥100		
	アイスティー （レモン・ミルク）	(S) ¥100	(M) ¥180	(L) ¥200
	アイスコーヒー	(S) ¥100	(L) ¥200	
	シェイク（バニラ・ 　ストロベリー・ 　チョコレート）	(S) ¥100	(L) ¥200	
	ホットドリンク			
	ホットティー （レモン・ミルク）	¥180		
	ブレンドコーヒー	(S) ¥100	(L) ¥200	
	ホットココア	¥180		

サイドメニュー				
	サラダ	¥200		
	フライドポテト	(S) ¥100	(M) ¥250	(L) ¥300
	チキンナゲット	¥200		

セットメニュー			
	ハンバーガーセット	¥600	ドリンク ＆ フライドポテト
	ビッグバーガーセット	¥630	ドリンク ＆ フライドポテト
	チーズバーガーセット	¥630	ドリンク ＆ フライドポテト
	ダブルチーズバーガーセット	¥640	ドリンク ＆ フライドポテト
	テリヤキバーガーセット	¥630	ドリンク ＆ フライドポテト
	テリヤキチキンバーガーセット	¥640	ドリンク ＆ フライドポテト
	フィッシュバーガーセット	¥640	ドリンク ＆ フライドポテト

1. How much is a teriyaki burger? ....

2. How much is a medium-sized cola? ....

3. How much are medium-sized French fries? ....

4. How much is a fish burger with a drink and French fries as a set menu"? ....

8 Match the kanji characters in box on the left with the readings in the box on the right. You can find the answers on page 127.

1. 月
2. 林
3. 耳
4. 金
5. 白

a. はやし
b. つき
c. みみ
d. しろ
e. きん

9 The following are stations on the Yamanote Line in Tokyo. Fill in the boxes with appropriate kanji. You can find the answers on page 127.

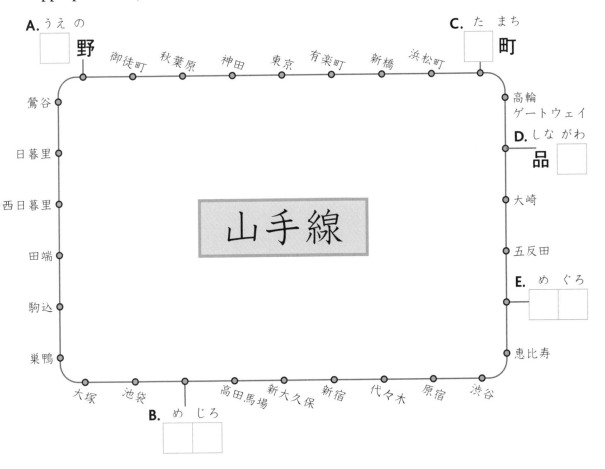

🎧 **10** Read the following passage written by Tadashi Yamaguchi regarding his favorite hobby, which is cooking. Some furigana are provided. Use the audio to check the accuracy of your pronunciation. You can find the English translation on page 127.

ぼくの趣味は料理をすることです。ひまなときは料理をします。日本料理が好きです。よくてんぷらを作ります。金曜日の晩はうちで友達といっしょにご飯を食べます。みんな喜びます。

山口　正

🎧 **11** Read the following passage written by Yoko Kawakami regarding her favorite hobby, which is watching movies. Some furigana are provided. Use the audio to check the accuracy of your pronunciation. You can find the English translation on page 127.

私の趣味は映画を見ることです。いろいろな映画を見ます。映画館で新しい映画を見るのが好きです。アメリカ映画が大好きです。

川上　陽子

Vocabulary

ぼく		I / me (male)
趣味	しゅみ	hobby
料理をする	りょうりをする	to cook
ひまなとき		free time
日本料理	にほんりょうり	Japanese food
好きです	すきです	to like
よく		often
作ります	つくります	to make
晩	ばん	evening
うちで		at home
友達	ともだち	friend(s)

と		with
いっしょに		together
ご飯	ごはん	meal
みんな		everyone
喜びます	よろこびます	to be happy
私	わたし	I / me
映画	えいが	movie(s)
いろいろな		various
映画館	えいがかん	cinema
新しい	あたらしい	new
大好きです	だいすきです	to really like

Appendix I: Examples of commonly used radicals

1 偏 (へん) ▢ Left

Radical	Name of radical	Example vocabulary word
イ	にんべん person	休む（やすむ）to rest
彳	ぎょうにんべん road, walking	行く（いく）to go
木	きへん tree	桜（さくら）cherry tree
禾	のぎへん grain	稲（いね）rice plant
日	ひへん sun, day	明るい（あかるい）bright
女	おんなへん woman	嫁（よめ）bride
氵	さんずいへん water	海（うみ）ocean
食	しょくへん eat, food	飲む（のむ）to drink
糸	いとへん thread / tie	細い（ほそい）thin
弓	ゆみへん bow	引く（ひく）to pull, draw
阝	こざとへん hill / mound	陸（りく）land
馬	うまへん horse	駅（えき）railway station
魚	さかなへん fish	鮪（まぐろ）tuna
扌	てへん hand	持つ（もつ）to hold
犭	けものへん animal	猿（さる）monkey
牛	うしへん cow, bull	物（もの）thing
青	あおへん blue	静か（しずか）quiet
釒	かねへん metal, money, gold	銀（ぎん）silver
訁	ごんべん say, word	語（ご）words
足	あしへん foot, leg, move	跳ぶ（とぶ）to jump
耳	みみへん listen	聴く（きく）to listen (carefully)
土	つちへん soil, earth, plant	塩（しお）salt
子	こどもへん child	孔（あな）hole
口	くちへん mouth	吸う（すう）to suck
車	くるまへん vehicle	軽い（かるい）light (in weight)
冫	にすい ice, freeze	凍る（こおる）to freeze
月	つきへん, にくづき moon, body	胸（むね）chest (body part)

2 冠 (かんむり) ▢ Top

Radical	Name of radical	Example vocabulary word
艹	くさかんむり grass	花 （はな） flower
宀	うかんむり roof	家 （いえ） house
亠	なべぶた lid	交じる （まじる） to mix / cross
雨	あめかんむり rain	雪 （ゆき） snow
罒	あみがしら eye, net	罪 （つみ） sin
竹	たけかんむり bamboo	筆 （ふで） brush for writing
冖	わかんむり cover, roof	冠 （かんむり） crown
穴	あなかんむり hole, opening	窓 （まど） window
⺍	つかんむり small	巣 （す） nest
山	やまかんむり mountain	嵐 （あらし） storm

3 脚 (あし) ▢ Bottom

Radical	Name of radical	Example vocabulary word
灬	よつてん fire	煮る （にる） to cook
儿	ひとあし person's legs	兄 （あに） older brother
心	こころ heart / mind	思う （おもう） to think
夂	なつあし slow movement	夏 （なつ） summer

4 旁 (つくり) ▢ Right

Radical	Name of radical	Example vocabulary word
斤	おのづくり ax, chop, cut	断る （ことわる） to refuse
隹	ふるとり bird	難しい （むずかしい） difficult
力	ちから strength	動く （うごく） to move
彡	さんづくり hairs, delicate	形 （かたち） shape
寸	すんづくり hand, measure	対 （つい） counter for sets (of clothes, small furniture, things, etc.)
欠	けんづくり gape, open mouth	次 （つぎ） next
頁	おおがい head, mind, face	顔 （かお） face
殳	ほこづくり strike, use tool	殺す （ころす） to kill
阝	おおざと village, town	都 （みやこ） capital city

5 構 (かまえ) ▢ ◫ ◡ ◱ ◲ Outside

Radical	Name of radical	Example vocabulary word
口	くにがまえ border	国 （くに） country
門	もんがまえ gate	間 （あいだ） in-between
凵	うけばこ container, vessel	凶 （きょう） bad
匚	かくしがまえ container	区 （く） ward (area of a city)
ク	つつみがまえ cover, protect	包む （つつむ） to wrap

6 垂 (たれ) ◰ Left and top

疒	やまいだれ sickness	病 （やまい） sickness
广	まだれ building	庭 （にわ） garden, yard
尸	しかばねだれ corpse, building	尾 （お） tail
戸	とだれ door, building	扉 （とびら） door

7 繞 (にょう) ◳ Left and bottom

辶	しんにょう movement, road	道 （みち） road
廴	えんにょう movement	建てる （たてる） to build

Appendix II: Handwritten characters

Some Japanese typefaces place a particular emphasis on certain parts of a stroke. Some typefaces connect different parts of the strokes. The charts on this page show you how handwritten characters usually appear.

Hiragana

あ	い	う	え	お
か	き	く	け	こ
さ	し	す	せ	そ
た	ち	つ	て	と
な	に	ぬ	ね	の
は	ひ	ふ	へ	ほ
ま	み	む	め	も
や		ゆ		よ
ら	り	る	れ	ろ
わ	を	ん		

Katakana

ア	イ	ウ	エ	オ
カ	キ	ク	ケ	コ
サ	シ	ス	セ	ソ
タ	チ	ツ	テ	ト
ナ	ニ	ヌ	ネ	ノ
ハ	ヒ	フ	ヘ	ホ
マ	ミ	ム	メ	モ
ヤ		ユ		ヨ
ラ	リ	ル	レ	ロ
ワ	ヲ	ン		

Kanji

一	二	三	四	五
山	川	木	林	田
口	目	足	手	耳
上	下	右	左	中
百	千	万	円	金
月	火	水	土	日
見	行	食	飲	書
赤	白	青	黒	黄
大	小	高	安	明
男	女	人	子	犬

Appendix III: Photocopiable practice sheet

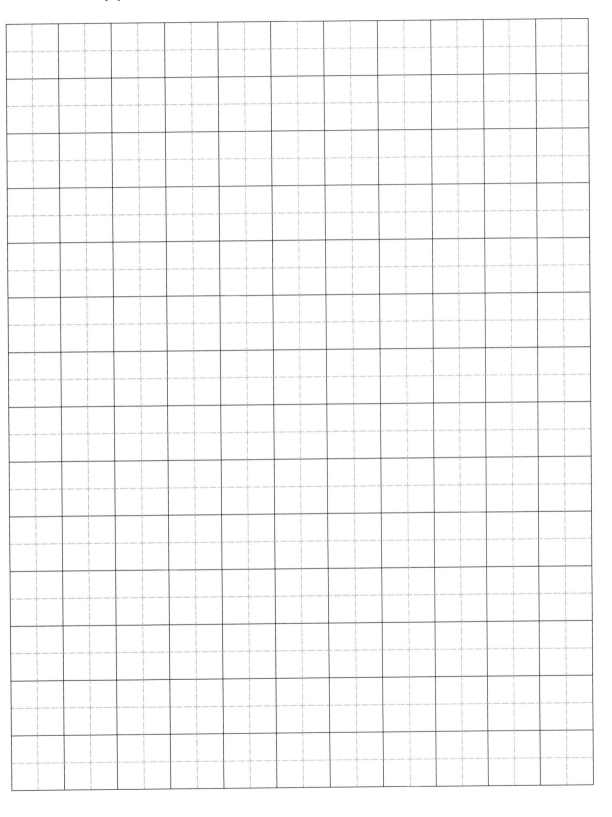

Answer key

Part One: The Hiragana Alphabet

Page 17

E 1. いえ (**ie**, house) 2. うえ (**ue**, up) 3. あい (**ai**, love)

Page 19

E 1. かき (**kaki**, persimmon) 2. こい (**koi**, carp) 3. きく (**kiku**, chrysanthemum)

Page 21

E 1. すいか (**suika**, watermelon 2. かさ (**kasa**, umbrella) 3. あし (**ashi**, foot / leg)

Page 23

E 1. つき (**tsuki**, the moon) 2. たこ (**tako**, octopus) 3. つくえ (**tsukue**, desk)

Page 25

E 1. にく (**niku**, meat) 2. きのこ (**kinoko**, mushroom) 3. さかな (**sakana**, fish)

Page 27

E 1. はし (**hashi**, chopsticks) 2. はし (**hashi**, bridge) 3. ふね (**fune**, boat)
(1. and 2. differ only in pitch accent.)

Page 29

E 1. かめ (**kame**, turtle) 2. うま (**uma**, horse) 3. くも (**kumo**, spider)

Page 31

E 1. やま (**yama**, mountain) 2. やさい (**yasai**, vegetable) 3. おゆ (**oyu**, hot water)

Page 33

E 1. くるま (**kuruma**, car) 2. あり (**ari**, ant) 3. さくら (**sakura**, cherry [tree or flower])

Page 35

D 1. かわ (**kawa**, river) 2. わたあめ (**wata-ame**, cotton candy) 3. きんこ (**kinko**, safe)

Page 37

D 1. ごみ (**gomi**, trash) 2. ことば (**kotoba**, words, language) 3. かんぱい (**kanpai**, toast [with drinks])
4. がいこく (**gaikoku**, foreign country) 5. こんぶ (**konbu**, kelp)
6. てんぷする (**tenpu suru**, to attach [file to an email])

Page 39

E 1. けっこん (**kekkon**, marriage) 2. おとうと (**otōto**, little brother) 3. いもうと (**imōto**, little sister)
4. かわいい (**kawaī**, cute) 5. べんとう (**bentō**, boxed lunch)
6. びっくりする (**bikkuri suru**, to be surprised)

Page 41

D 1. しゃしん (**shashin**, photo) 2. でんしゃ (**densha**, train) 3. ちゅうごく (**chūgoku**, China)
4. びょういん (**byōin**, hospital) 5. きゅうりょう (**kyūryō**, salary) 6. ゆにゅう (**yunyū**, import)

Page 43

1. め (**me**, eyes) 2. くち (**kuchi**, mouth) 3. みみ (**mimi**, ears) 4. はな (**hana**, nose) 5. て (**te**, hands / arms)
6. あし (**ashi**, feet / legs)

Page 45

Samuku narimashita ga, Yamada-san wa o-genki desu ka. Kochira mina, genki ni shite imasu. Hanako wa ima, kōkōsei desu. "Hayaku daigaku ni nyūgaku shitai." to itte imasu. Mainichi furūto to kurarinetto no renshū o shite imasu.

The weather has turned cold, I hope you are well, Yamada-san. We are all well here. Hanako is a high school student now. "I want to go to university soon," she says. She practices flute and clarinet every day.

Page 46

A Hajimemashite. Watashi no namae wa Mori Junko desu. Yoroshiku onegaishimasu.

How do you do. My name is Junko Mori. Nice to meet you.

Part Two: The Katakana Alphabet

Page 51

E 1. アイロン iron   2. エプロン apron   3. オーブン oven

Page 53

E 1. コアラ koala   2. カメラ camera   3. ケーキ cake

Page 55

D 1. サングラス sunglasses   2. スカーフ scarf   3. セーター sweater

Page 57

D 1. タイヤ tire   2. チケット ticket   3. テレビ TV

Page 59

D 1. ナイフ knife   2. ネクタイ necktie   3. ネックレス necklace

Page 61

D 1. ハンバーガー hamburger   2. ピアノ piano   3. ホルン French horn

Page 63

D 1. メロン melon   2. メトロノーム metronome   3. マイク microphone

Page 65

D 1. ヨーグルト yogurt   2. ヨガ yoga   3. ヨット yacht

Page 67

D 1. ライター lighter   2. レモン lemon   3. ロッカー locker

Page 69

D 1. ワイン wine   2. ワッフル waffle   3. ワイパー windshield wiper

Page 73

B 1. レタス lettuce   2. クラリネット clarinet   3. テニス tennis   4. クッキー cookies
5. オレンジジュース orange juice

Page 75

D 1. Marilyn Monroe   2. George Washington   3. William Shakespeare   4. Oprah Winfrey
5. Awkwafina   6. Elon Musk

Part Three: Kanji

Page 104

A 1. ひへん 2. しんにょう 3. くさかんむり 4. ちから 5. ひとあし 6. くにがまえ 7. やまいだれ

Page 105

B

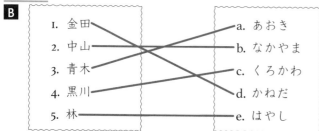

山	mountain	涙	tears	病気	illness	海	ocean
川	river	河	river	湖	lake	明るい	bright
林	woods	お酒	liquor	港	harbor	漁	fishing
田	rice paddy	金	gold	黒	black	青	blue
漢字	kanji	泳ぐ	to swim	洗う	to wash	洪水	flooding

Page 107

B

1. 金田 — d. かねだ
2. 中山 — b. なかやま
3. 青木 — a. あおき
4. 黒川 — c. くろかわ
5. 林 — e. はやし

Page 111

A
1. **Yama to kawa** — Mountains and rivers
2. **Hidari to migi** — Left and right
3. **Ue to shita** — Up and down
4. **Me to kuchi** — Eye and mouth
5. **Te to ashi** — Hand and leg
6. **Kore wa takai desu.** — This is expensive.
7. **Ano yama o mite kudasai. Totemo takai yama desu.** — Please look at that mountain. It's a really high mountain.
8. **Kore wa san man en desu. Are wa go sen en desu.** — This is 30,000 yen. That's 5,000 yen.
9. **Ano otoko no hito wa Aoki-san desu.** — That man is Aoki-san.
   Ano onna no hito wa Kobayashi-san desu. — That woman is Kobayashi-san.
10. **Miso shiru o nomimashita. Sore kara, sushi o tabemashita.** — I had miso soup. Then I had sushi.
11. **Watashi no kaban wa akai desu. Ōyama-san no wa kuroi desu.** — My bag is red. Oyama-san's is black.

Review

Page 114

2

う	な	ぎ	く	す
ま	す	は	に	き
さ	し	み	な	や
み	そ	し	る	き
う	て	ん	ぷ	ら

Page 115

4

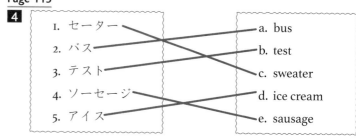

1. セーター — c. sweater
2. バス — a. bus
3. テスト — b. test
4. ソーセージ — e. sausage
5. アイス — d. ice cream

5
1. エジプト　　Egypt
2. イタリア　　Italy
3. カナダ　　　Canada
4. タイ　　　　Thailand
5. アメリカ　　USA
6. スペイン　　Spain
7. ドイツ　　　Germany
8. イギリス　　England
9. インド　　　India
10. チリ　　　　Chile
11. オーストラリア　Australia
12. フランス　　France
13. ブラジル　　Brazil
14. ロシア　　　Russia

6

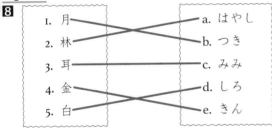

7 1. 280 yen,　2. 180 yen,　3. 250 yen,　4. 640 yen

8
1. 月　　　　a. はやし
2. 林　　　　b. つき
3. 耳　　　　c. みみ
4. 金　　　　d. しろ
5. 白　　　　e. きん

9 A. 上　B. 目白　C. 田　D. 川　E. 目黒

10 Boku no shumi wa ryōri o suru koto desu. Hima na toki wa ryōri o shimasu. Nihon-ryōri ga suki desu. Yoku tenpura o tsukurimasu. Kinyōbi no ban wa uchi de tomodachi to issho ni gohan o tabemasu. Minna yorokobimasu. Yamaguchi Tadashi

My hobby is cooking. When I'm free, I cook. I like Japanese food. I often make tempura. On Friday evenings I have a meal with my friends at my house. We are all happy. Tadashi Yamaguchi

11 Watashi no shumi wa eiga o miru koto desu. Iroiro na eiga o mimasu. Eigakan de atarashii eiga o miru no ga suki desu. Amerika-eiga ga dai suki desu. Kawakami Yōko

My hobby is watching movies. I watch various kinds of movies. I like watching new movies at the cinema. I like American movies. Yoko Kawakami

"Books to Span the East and West"

Tuttle Publishing was founded in 1832 in the small New England town of Rutland, Vermont [USA]. Our core values remain as strong today as they were then—to publish best-in-class books which bring people together one page at a time. In 1948, we established a publishing office in Japan—and Tuttle is now a leader in publishing English-language books about the arts, languages and cultures of Asia. The world has become a much smaller place today and Asia's economic and cultural influence has grown. Yet the need for meaningful dialogue and information about this diverse region has never been greater. Over the past seven decades, Tuttle has published thousands of books on subjects ranging from martial arts and paper crafts to language learning and literature—and our talented authors, illustrators, designers and photographers have won many prestigious awards. We welcome you to explore the wealth of information available on Asia at www.tuttlepublishing.com.

Published by Tuttle Publishing, an imprint of Periplus Editions (HK) Ltd.

www.tuttlepublishing.com

Copyright © 2021 by Periplus Editions (HK) Ltd.
Cover illustration by Dragana Gordic. Illustration page 12 by imtmphoto. Both Shutterstock.

All rights reserved.

Library of Congress Catalog-in-Publication Data in progress

ISBN 978-4-8053-1658-0

First edition, 2021

Distributed by
North America, Latin America & Europe
Tuttle Publishing
364 Innovation Drive
North Clarendon,
VT 05759-9436 U.S.A.
Tel: 1 (802) 773-8930
Fax: 1 (802) 773-6993
info@tuttlepublishing.com
www.tuttlepublishing.com

Japan
Tuttle Publishing
Yaekari Building, 3rd Floor,
5-4-12 Osaki, Shinagawa-ku,
Tokyo 141 0032
Tel: (81) 3 5437-017
Fax: (81) 3 5437-0755
sales@tuttle.co.jp
www.tuttle.co.jp

Asia Pacific
Berkeley Books Pte. Ltd.
3 Kallang Sector #04-01
Singapore 349278
Tel: (65) 6741-2178
Fax: (65) 6741-2179
inquiries@periplus.com.sg
www.tuttlepublishing.com

25 24 23 22 21   5 4 3 2 1

Printed in Malaysia   2108VP

TUTTLE PUBLISHING® is a registered trademark of Tuttle Publishing, a division of Periplus Editions (HK) Ltd.